NOT WITHOUT RISK

About the Author

Pete Trewin was born in Middlesbrough under the shadow of the steel mills but has lived for most of his life in a leafy suburb of Liverpool with his wife, Paula and golden retriever, Eira. Their three children have long moved on.

While working as an economic development and regeneration consultant, Pete gained a knowledge of how you might launder ill-gotten money. Not direct experience, obviously. This set him on the path of writing crime novels. The rest of his time is spent in Snowdonia where he indulges his interest in rock climbing and hill walking.

Other books by Pete Trewin: *A Fair Wack, Time Lapse*

NOT WITHOUT RISK

Pete Trewin

For Paula

CHAPTER ONE

Martin Bennett turned a corner and the hospital came into view. He stopped for a moment to catch his breath. His mouth felt dry and sweat ran down his cheeks. The grey concrete used in the Sixties to construct the monstrosity of a building looked like the end result of some poisonous industrial process. It reminded him of the dumped slag that used to form mountains and cliffs down by the river at Widnes.

He slung his satchel around his back and walked on past a huge hoarding showing the proposed new hospital. The blue sky in the artist's sketch matched the cloudless sky above. A red strip about two feet wide stretched across the main pedestrian access. On it in big white letters: *No smoking beyond this point.* Outside the entrance, a crowd of smokers, some in hospital gowns and carrying drips, puffed away. He pushed through the crowd and went in. His hands trembled.

Inside, he followed endless corridors. Fluorescent lights overhead, blue lino underfoot, pine-veneered doors leading off. Messages on the lino. Combinations of the words *Commitment, Compassion, Communication, Care.*

He got a surprise when he reached the waiting room for the cardiac clinic. He'd expected the patients to be overweight and unhealthy, but everyone looked average. Like him.

An old man, completely bald and looking more like a skeleton than a living person, sat slumped in a wheelchair. He seemed to be asleep but muttered quietly to himself. Martin recalled reading George Orwell's essay 'How the Poor Die' one sunny afternoon in the Park Lane flat. Hospitals under the British National Health Service were much nicer places now compared to French ones in the Twenties, but even so, a fear of hospitals persisted in the subconscious. He'd not read the essay for years, but the passage in which the old Frenchman cries out 'Je Pisse!' just before he expires in agony in a crowded, squalid ward felt very real to him at this moment.

The tests took most of the morning. Blood pressure. Scans. Leads stuck to his body and connected to a computer. Finally, a nurse laid him on his back and placed a metal contraption over his head and face—like Hannibal Lector's in the horror film—and he slid into a machine with background noises like the grinding of a broken gearbox on an old car. The nurse told him to tap on the side if he couldn't stand it, and only the fear of looking like a wuss stopped him from doing so.

'Do many people give in?' he asked after she'd pulled him out of the torture chamber and released him from the mask.

'Lots,' she replied with a grin on her face.

Back in the waiting room the receptionist summoned him in to meet the doctor. Young, Middle Eastern-looking. Striped shirt and fawn chinos. Brown brogues. 'Okay,

Mr Bennett,' the doctor said. 'Tell me what happened. I know you've told us before, but just go through it again.' He read the file notes as Martin spoke.

'I woke up with numbness in the right side of my body. I couldn't walk properly. Co-ordination things. Stubbed my toe on the end of the bed. At first I thought it was cramp in my leg. But then I noticed that I had difficulty writing.'

'Which side was this?'

'The right side. I'm right-handed.'

'Anything else?'

'That afternoon I was making a cup of tea in the kitchen when I saw these zigzag flashes across my eyes. Then it seemed like I was being taken by a huge, curving wave of greyness. Next thing I was on the floor.'

'Did you lose consciousness?'

'Momentarily.'

'Any pain?'

'No, just nausea.'

The doctor moved his chair close in front of Martin and held out his hands. 'I want you to hold my hands and push.' The doctor pushed against him with surprising strength. Martin pushed back. The doctor let him go, then watched his face. 'Smile,' he said.

Martin complied.

'Any problems with speech?'

'No.'

He nodded and moved his chair back to the desk. 'Any other symptoms?'

'No.'

The doctor nodded. 'That's good.' He opened a drawer and got out a piece of paper. 'Now, if you'll just answer a few questions. Who is the Queen of England?'

'Elizabeth the Second.'

'What year is it now?'

'2016.'

'What month is it?'

'May.'

'Repeat this phrase: John Brown, 4 West Road, Childwall.'

Martin did so.

'What time is it, roughly?'

'About ten thirty?'

'Now count backwards from twenty to one.'

Martin had to concentrate on fourteen to thirteen but he managed it.

'Now say the months of the year in reverse order.'

Martin stumbled on August to July but again managed it.

'Now repeat the address I gave you earlier.'

'John Brown, 4 West Road, Childwall.'

'Excellent.' The doctor totted up the score. 'Top marks. Well done. Now, Mr Bennett. We've had a chance to look at all the scans, and we've had a conference. As you know, the question is: do we operate or not? Well, we've decided that you don't necessarily have to have it. It's up to you. The operation is not without risk, and we think that you can get by with increased medication to lower your blood pressure and cholesterol levels. We can hold off the operation for the time being if you agree.'

A wave of relief passed through Martin's body, washing away the tension and anxiety. He grinned at the doctor.

'Hang on,' the doctor said, 'before you start doing back flips. You'll have to take things easy. Take a couple of weeks off work. Do some gardening. Change your lifestyle. It says here that you are a non-smoker and a moderate drinker. Right? You seem like a tense person, if I may say so, so relax. Take some gentle exercise—a brisk walk, say—every day. You could do with losing some weight, if you don't mind me saying so. No driving, of course. And definitely no stress.' He made a note. 'Are you married? Do you have a family?'

Martin thought about this. 'Not really,' he said at last. 'My parents are dead. No brothers or sisters. I'm divorced. We have a daughter, but she's grown up.' He paused, aware that he sounded like a saddo. 'This operation. It's not without risk? What kind of risk are we talking about?'

'Not a great risk. Two per cent.'

'And the risk is?'

'Death.'

Two percent. That didn't sound too bad. Two in a hundred. But he'd passed maybe a hundred people in the corridors on the way in. Two of them sounded different.

'I'll go with the no operation option,' he said.

The doctor grinned and clapped his hands. 'Excellent! Now take this as your chance to make a new start. Change your lifestyle.' He leaned forward and clasped both of Martin's hands in his, suddenly serious. 'I see a lot of men your age. They don't listen. Can I give you some advice, Mr Bennett? Seize the day, Mr Bennett, seize the day!'

*

Outside the hospital, Martin took deep breaths of fresh air, like a prisoner on death row who has received a last-minute reprieve. His satchel bulged with a big package of various boxes of tablets that he'd collected from the pharmacy. An operation promised a lasting solution, but the risk was real. He'd made the right decision. He stepped into a pall of cigarette smoke and wafted his hand in front of his face. It reminded him of the old days when they allowed smoking in pubs. He was dying for a fag, but his new lifestyle had to start somewhere. He took out the packet of fags he'd bought in case he'd been handed a death sentence—then he would have started again—and, without looking, handed it to someone in the crowd. 'Here y'are, mate,' he said.

A few steps later someone grabbed his arm.

'Martin? Martin Bennett?'

He turned. A gap-toothed man held Martin's fag packet in his hand.

'It's John Hardin,' the man shouted. 'I've not seen you in what ... twenty-five years!'

Martin raised an eyebrow. 'John; it's nice to see you again.'

He didn't say that John Hardin looked different. Totally different. The golden locks were gone. He was almost bald, and what he had left was grey. He seemed to have shrunk in height from his previous six feet so that his eyes were level with Martin's. He was thinner, almost emaciated; the bones in his once handsome face stretched the skin as if they wanted to escape. And the John Hardin he'd known all those years ago would have had the silly-looking gap in his front teeth fixed—he'd been so vain. He must be hard up.

'Come on,' John said. 'Let's have a coffee and rap about the old days!'

'Fine,' Martin said. 'You lead the way.'

Martin's smile masked his real feelings. For years he'd dreamt of causing severe pain to the man who had destroyed his marriage. Not kill him. That would be wrong. But Martin had wanted him to suffer some pain so he'd understand what it felt like.

John led him to the atrium at the top of the escalator, a bright, busy space that looked out onto a parade of nondescript shops. Martin followed him into a dark, cave-like coffee bar in a corner.

'What's yours?' Martin asked as they approached the counter. 'You go and sit down.'

'Americano, no milk, no sugar.'

Martin had the same.

He placed the cups of coffee on the table and sat next to John in a small alcove. Low conversation buzzed and crockery rattled in the background. 'So how's things?' he asked. 'I thought you were in America?'

John grinned, pale and ghostly in the subdued light. The lines on his face merged so his jaw appeared separate from the rest of his face, like on a wooden puppet. The effect was so startling compared to the memory of almost impossible good looks that, for a second, Martin felt physical revulsion. With his open mouth revealing bad teeth and gaps, John looked worse than Martin ever had. So there was some justice in the world.

The malice rising from somewhere deep inside himself—somewhere he didn't know or denied existed—surprised Martin.

'Oh, things didn't quite work out as I'd planned.' John laughed. 'So what are you in here for?' An American drawl overlaid John's St Helens accent.

'A stroke. And you?'

'Liver's destroyed. Drunk too much pop. And my shit's fucked up. Do you know that Warren Zevon song? *Well, I went to the doctor ...*' He sang loudly, causing nearby customers to turn and stare. '*I said I'm feeling kind of rough. He said, let me break it to you, son. Your shit's fucked up.*'

His voice caught on the last word, and he went into a coughing fit. He got out a small black container, shook out a little black sweet and popped it in his mouth. He offered the container to Martin, who caught a whiff of menthol and turned away.

'Fancy an Imp?' Hardin said. 'All this medication makes my throat go dry.'

'Imps? I haven't seen them for years. I didn't realise that you could still get them.'

'Yeah. There's a little shop by the St John's precinct. They specialise in sweets from the past. Want one?'

'No thanks. So your shit's fucked up. What's changed?

You always were full of shit.'

'Ha, very true. Still climbing?'

'A bit.' Martin took a sip of his coffee.

'Still dropping people?'

'Come on, I never dropped you. I burnt my hands trying to stop you.'

'It took me six months for my ankle to knit together again after that fall. Mind you, I thought you were a goner when you fell off that path.'

Martin felt himself blushing. They'd been walking down the path from a climb. He'd turned to reply to something John had said. He must have stepped on some mud or wet leaves or something, and he'd gone arse over tit over the crag. By some miracle the thick vegetation at the bottom had stopped his fall, but he'd been stunned and covered with cuts and bruises. Nothing broken. Incredibly lucky.

'What about,' Martin said, 'when you abbed off the end of the rope into the sea at Gogarth?'

It was John's turn to blush. 'Lucky I'm a strong swimmer. Though I nearly got dragged under by the weight of the gear. What about when you fell off at Cloggy? You went off screaming into the mist and came back half an hour later, still screaming.'

'They had to cut my strides off me back at the hut.'

'And the time we were top roping at Helsby. I was about to fall off, shouting "tight rope!" to you at the top. Or where I thought you were. I looked down, and there you were at the bottom. You bastard.' John leaned back in his chair.

'Good times,' he said. 'I haven't climbed for years. Can't abide all these bolts, mats and climbing walls. Remember what they used to say: respect the rock? It's not a proper sport now; it's a leisure pastime people do to keep fit. Remember what Hemingway said? "There are only three true sports, the rest are games."'

'Motor racing.' Martin remembered the same conversation from years before. 'Bull fighting and mountaineering.' He'd never been sure about the bull fighting. The odds were pretty much stacked against the bull. 'You have to risk your life in a true sport.' He shrugged and smiled. 'People want to survive, not kill themselves. Not everyone wants to fight a bull or race fast cars around all the time. I bet you're not climbing now.'

John laughed. 'No, I'm not. Got a family? Kids?'

Martin nodded. 'One girl.' He looked away. 'Julie and I split up.'

'Sorry to hear that. Same thing happened to me. Seems to be the way these days, doesn't it? I had a business in the States. I was doing all right. Then I had some bad luck. It went bust and everything just went tits up. Had to come back over here.'

'Living in Liverpool?'

John nodded. 'Gambier Terrace.'

'One of Liverpool's landmarks, that. Gumshoe. The Beatles.'

'I knew that one of the Beatles lived there. But what was Gumshoe?'

'A Sixties film. Albert Finney. About this bingo caller

who gets mixed up in murder and stuff. Kind of a scouse noir movie.'

John nodded. 'I'll have to check it out.'

'You can't get it at normal outlets. You'd have to get it off the internet.'

'Right.' He leaned back in his seat and grinned at Martin. 'This is just like being back in Park Lane in that flat with you and Lester—smoking dope, dropping acid and listening to records. Those were good days, weren't they?'

A long silence.

'Look,' John said at last, the grin gone. 'I'm sorry for what happened. I've got to bail.' He stood and walked away, leaving his mobile and a bunch of keys on the table.

'John,' Martin shouted after him, but John kept walking.

Martin studied the keys. The cardboard on the tab read *Flat 9A*.

Looks like an estate agent's tab. Can't have lived there long.

He slung his satchel on his back, grabbed the keys and the mobile, and ran after John to the top of the escalator. John stood halfway down with a hooded figure behind him. He or she moved out to pass him, appeared to pat John on the back, then ran down the escalator and out of view. John slumped onto the escalator and slid off onto the floor at the bottom.

It was all a blur, over in an instant. Had it really happened?

Martin ran down the escalator, stumbled off at the end and knelt by the slumped figure. John turned towards him. His face looked like a skull on which parchment had been stretched.

'I've had it, kid,' he whispered.

'Who did it, John? That was a professional hit.'

'Don't get mixed up in it, kid.' His eyes opened wide. 'Oh, fuck!' His head banged onto the floor, and it seemed as if his whole body deflated a little. Like a balloon being let down. He lay there, not moving.

Martin stepped back. Unable to think straight, he turned and walked as calmly as he could to the exit. He had to get some fresh air. Outside, he walked to a railing and held onto it, breathing deeply. He bent over, had to grab his satchel as it swung around, and realised he still clutched Hardin's keys and mobile. He unzipped the side pocket of the satchel and slipped them inside, then zipped it back up.

Shouldn't he go back? He couldn't just leave him. For years he'd dreamed of giving John Hardin some pain. Punch him hard in the mouth. Wipe the stupid grin off his face. Now he'd seen him murdered. Hardin had deserved what he'd got, but it didn't seem right, almost as if he, Martin Bennett, was somehow implicated. But it had nothing to do with him.

A babble of raised voices and shouts came from inside the hospital. In the distance a police siren drew closer. Too late.

CHAPTER TWO

Amy collared Martin at the main entrance to the office and pulled him into the entrance to the stairs, closing the door behind them. She must have followed him in.

In the gloom of the stairwell, Amy's dyed blonde hair contrasted with her bright red lipstick. 'We've got problems with the Irish Streets,' she whispered as if they were conspirators in some plot. Her pugnacity made up for her small size.

Still in shock, he mumbled something. He was going to be sick.

'The residents have put in another objection,' she said. 'I actually agree with them. Those houses are too good to demolish.'

He sighed. 'Amy, I agree with you, but we're paid to make the project happen. You know what Lester will say.'

'I know very well what he'll say. It'll be the old chestnut about China. How they just get on with building dams while in India they have democracy so the dams don't get built and the country has no power. I've heard it a hundred times. But then in India they save their historic areas, and in China they raze them to the ground. There're two sides to every argument like this.'

She paused.

He shrugged and looked away.

'So we're just paid hands doing what the boss says?' she said at last.

'Yes.'

She tilted her head. 'I know you two are as thick as thieves and that this is probably a mistake.' She took a deep breath. 'But Lester's worse. He's become a liability. Watches his You Tube videos and listens to his music all day. Doesn't do any work and is rude to clients. The way it's going we'll be on the rocks again. Remember what happened last time. And we're in the middle of a recession.'

'Is it the pop?'

'Yeah,' she said, her voice full of sarcasm.

'Look, Amy,' he said. 'I'm not well. I'm afraid I'm going to have to go on leave for a while.'

'I heard that you weren't well. But it's just getting on top of me at the moment.'

'Look, I'll try and help as much as possible, but you're going to have to lead the project. E-mail me the latest stuff and I'll have a look at it.'

'And Lester?'

Martin shrugged. 'He's the boss.'

*

'John Hardin? Dead?' Lester Adams stared at Martin. At six foot two—Lester didn't hold with metric measurements—and seventeen stone, he stood at least five stone heavier and four inches taller than Martin. Big face. Big features. Big hair—long, swept back and black but with grey streaks. Larger than life, like a cartoon of himself. He laughed. 'Come on, you're pulling my leg, old bean.'

'Nope. It's true. Have you got a glass of water? It was a bit of a shock.'

'Of course; you sit down. You shouldn't be having shocks in your condition.' He brought a glass of water, watched Martin as he drank, then walked across the office to look out of the window, which stretched almost to the floor. 'How did it happen?'

'I had the appointment at the hospital to discuss the stroke—'

'How did that go?'

'Oh, they told me to slow down—the usual. No need for surgery; they can handle it with medication. Told me to take a couple of weeks off work.'

'No operation? That's great! Sorry; go on about John.'

'Nothing much to say. We met. Had a cup of coffee, talked about old times.' Martin thought for a moment. Best not mention the figure on the escalator. 'He left. He was going down the escalator when he had a heart attack.'

'A hospital escalator?'

'Yeah. Ridiculous, isn't it? He certainly didn't look like the golden boy any more. More like a down-and-out.'

'Well, I know it's not good to talk ill of the dead, but he had it coming. I hated him.'

The depth of Lester's heart-felt words surprised Martin. It wasn't like him. Martin said nothing.

'Look,' Lester said after a long silence. 'Just forget

about John Hardin.' He smiled. 'Did the sawbones tell you to get more exercise?'

'As a matter of fact, he did. As you can see'—Martin patted his belly—'I've let myself go.'

'Well, my quack says the same. Says I like the good things in life too much. How about we do some running and climbing like in the old days?'

'Well, yes, but …'

'But what?' Lester grinned. 'Scared I'll whup your ass like I used to, old boy?' He laughed. 'Only joking, me old mucker. Look, take some time off. Your sabbatical starts now. I'll be over tomorrow morning so we can go for a run. Start as we mean to go on. Anyone can get fit. Just put down the cream cake and the sugary drink, get up off the sofa and run up the stairs a few times.'

'What if you live in a bungalow?'

'Ho, ho. You know what I mean. The future starts now. Seize the day.' He thought for a moment. 'Take two weeks off. Amy will look after things. She's very efficient. Here, have a look at this.' He handed Martin a file. 'I need someone to do some blue sky thinking on how the housing chapter in the Draft Merseyside Growth Strategy can be tightened up. Everything's on the table. Look at the green belt, for instance. See if there's any scope for releasing some land.' He frowned. 'Why the long face, Marty? Think outside the box for a change. When you've had a chance to chill out, read it and tell me what you think. And don't show it to anyone. Especially politicians and bad boys. Planning means cash in these parts. And it means a lot to people. Developing green fields, cutting down trees, demolishing perfectly good houses.' He laughed. 'But I don't need to tell you that, do I, Marty?'

He thought again. 'Here.' He handed over a thick wallet. Martin opened it. It was full of CDs. 'Remember when we were hippies and shared a flat all those years ago? I've made copies of some of the records we used to listen to. I was working on a funeral playlist.'

'Funeral playlist? For you or for me?'

'For me. But you might find it useful. The doctor said that if I didn't change my lifestyle I'd be up for the chop. Got me thinking. If I'm going to have a funeral, I want a good playlist. Get people tapping their feet. No doom and gloom. I don't want one of those funerals where everyone is sniffling. I'll leave a good wad for a good feed and piss up. You could do with a good playlist yourself by the sound of it. Go on, it'll help you relax.'

'This is a bit morbid, Lester. No one's going to die. I hope you're joking.'

Lester laughed.

*

Martin couldn't work. His mind kept roving around the events of the day. A reprieve from a death sentence. Meeting someone who'd ruined your life whom you'd not seen for thirty years. A murder in broad daylight. He'd have loved to go for a pint, a few pints, but no. He'd made the decision. Seize the day.

The satchel with John's mobile and keys sat at the side of his desk. He looked around. The office was deserted.

He put the satchel in the back of a drawer in an unused desk in the corner, then left.

On his way to the bus he took a short cut down an alley. At the end, just before the main road, a hand gripped his arm and a voice said in his ear, 'Could you spare a moment, sir?'

CHAPTER THREE

'Mr Bennett, my name is Detective Inspector O'Connor, and this is Detective Sergeant Robinson. You are under suspicion of leaving the scene of a crime. For all we know you could have been involved. Let's go through this again.'

O'Connnor had the short, steel-grey hair, square head and air of authority of a major in the US Marines. He could hardly have been more than forty, a good twenty years younger than Robinson, who smiled at Martin— big white tash under a mop of white hair—and motioned him to go on, pen poised over a notepad. Robinson's dark grey suit was in stark contrast to the maroon suit with wide lapels, pink shirt and pointy brown brogues that he usually wore in Martin's local pub. The harsh neon light highlighted the deep lines in his face. No secrets here. He'd obviously recognised Martin, too.

Martin sighed and gazed around the cramped police interview room. Bare walls, recently painted in institutional magnolia. Grey carpet. The only furniture a battered table and three chairs. The table's Formica surface must have been recently wiped clean, but he could still see the rings of ancient coffee stains and the ciggie burns from when smoking was allowed.

'I've been through it about six times,' he said. 'I hadn't seen John for twenty-five years when I met him outside the Royal. We used to climb together, then he went to America. I was at the hospital for an appointment to do with the stroke I had recently. We talked about old times for a few minutes, then John left. As he was going down the escalator, he collapsed. Someone behind him slapped him on the back.'

The two cops glanced at each other. 'Description of the attacker?' O'Connor said.

'It was all over in an instant. I didn't get a proper look. He was wearing a parka-type jacket with the hood up. Scarf covering the face.'

'Strange that no one else saw this person? We'll check the CCTV footage again, but the hospital have confirmed that Mr Hardin died of natural causes. A heart attack. Linked to his other health problems.' O'Connor studied Martin. 'So what was your involvement with Mr Hardin?'

'None at all. As I said, I hadn't seen him for twenty-five years. We met outside the hospital and we went inside to have a coffee. Talk about old times when we used to climb together. Why are you asking me all these questions? Was John involved in something?'

O'Connor stared at him. 'Mr Hardin was under surveillance. We have reason to believe that he was involved in illegal activities. You were the last person to see him alive. How do we know that you weren't involved in those activities?' He paused and smiled. 'If what you say is true, why did you make a run for it?'

'I was shocked. I panicked. We were sitting in the cafe and he just walked off. Must have been something I said. I went after him. What happened on the elevator was a shock. I panicked and just ran for it; like I said. I realise now it was the wrong thing to do. I was scared. I admit it doesn't sound very logical.'

O'Connor sighed. 'We could charge you with leaving the scene of a crime, and you would be a key witness. How would you like that?'

'Not a lot.'

'What was it you said you did for a living?'

'I work for a regeneration company, Development Solutions.'

'What's that when it's at home?'

'We carry out projects to regenerate Liverpool. Commissioned by the council, the mayor, people like that.'

'The aim being?'

'To create jobs, bring the city back to what it once was.'

O'Connor raised an eyebrow. 'You're not part of that crew who are demolishing perfectly good houses? What's it called, the Irish Streets?'

'It's not as simple as that—'

'It's quite simple, actually,' O'Connor said. 'Why not do them up for ordinary working class people to live in rather than demolish them and build yuppy houses?' He paused, then shoved his face forward so that it was only about six inches from Martin's. In the harsh, neon light, Martin saw the open pores on the man's nose. His hair looked like steel wool and even smelled metallic.

O'Connor stared into Martin's eyes. 'I'm not sure that I believe your story, Mr Bennett.' He banged his fist on the table. 'We had Mr Hardin under close surveillance and you show up. Bit of a coincidence that, don't you think? It'd be better for you if you owned up now. Was this a drop and he panicked? Where are his keys and his mobile? Where have you hidden them?'

'Look,' Martin said, 'I've told you the truth. Why are you treating me like some scally off the street?' He held the copper's stare for a moment before O'Connor pulled his face away and motioned to Robinson. They both left the room.

Martin sipped at the plastic cup of water he'd been given. Could they really charge him with anything? He was a professional man. A police record would end his career.

After five minutes, Robinson came back. His big face, with its large white tash under the mop of white hair, looked serious. He broke into a smile as he sat down. Bad cop, good cop.

'Well, Martin,' he said, 'we've rung your place of work. They've confirmed that you are employed there. And the hospital has confirmed that you had an appointment there today. We've checked the CCTV footage, and the camera is not in the best location for looking down that escalator. And there's a bit of glare from the natural light in the atrium. We think you made a mistake. John Hardin died of natural causes. The death's not suspicious, so the coroner won't be involved.'

'There is another person on the escalator with a hood over his head. But we can't identify him or her. It was a moving escalator so it is difficult to make out this person's height or build. From what we can make out he or she was about average. And you can't make out if they did anything to Mr Hardin. Probably just some random scally. Obviously not you. We can see you in the cafe and then at the top of the escalator.' He paused. 'So we've decided to be lenient this time. You are free to go. If anyone apart from us contacts you about this let us know at once.'

He reached in his jacket pocket and handed over a card, then rummaged in the other pocket. 'Oh, your belongings.' He handed over Martin's wallet and house keys and some loose change. They'd searched him. Routine, apparently. 'And don't talk to the press,' he added. 'They'll be swarming all over this story like flies. And please don't do anything foolish again. As the DI said, the sort of people who Mr Hardin was involved with are bad people. Any contact with them would be ... how can I put it? Not without risk.'

'What do you mean, bad people?' Martin asked.

Robinson sighed. 'I mean very bad people. Mr Hardin was involved in just about the dirtiest racket we've ever come across in this city.' He laughed at Martin's quizzical look. 'Well, that's enough for now. You're free to go. Just don't get involved in any of this shit. You can take that as a warning.'

Martin stood. 'I can absolutely confirm that I will not be having any contact with any bad people.'

'Might see you in The Black Horse.' Robinson's grin displayed a startling variety of yellow-stained, blackened and gold-filled teeth.

CHAPTER FOUR

Martin woke and reached for the ciggies. Not there.
Shit; he'd given them away. What a stupid thing to
do. He really needed a fag. Or a drink. A fag and a drink.
He lay still with his eyes shut, thinking. Bit of a headache,
dry mouth, unpleasant taste. No spit.

'You're a bag of shite,' he said out loud. 'A scumbag. A
deeply sad person. This is the first day of the rest of your
life. Seize the day!'

He got up, went downstairs in his T-shirt and underpants, emptied the gin into the sink and threw the bottle
into the bin. The clunk was satisfying. Forget about John
Hardin. Seize the day. He took the paper bag containing his new pills and went up to his bedroom. He sat on
the bed and spread the various packages out. Garish colours; orange and yellow. Strange-sounding names; Sim-
vastatin, Clopidogrel, Amlopidine, Ramipril. He took a
pill out of each box, popping them out of their bubbles,
swallowed the lot with a mouthful of water and went into
the back bedroom.

The awful floral wallpaper was coming off in huge
sheets, and he loved helping it on its way. Therapeutic.
But it wouldn't last long. The layer of paper underneath
had been painted with what looked like orange gloss

paint. You couldn't just soak it with water and scrape it off. You had to score it with a sharp blade first, and then it only came off in small bits. Must have been put on by some idiot of a hippy in the Sixties or Seventies.

High up by the ceiling, next to the chimney breast, the layer of paint and paper had blistered and it was easier to get off. He ran a hand over an area of plaster that'd been cleared and should have dried out by now. Damp. Must be a leak in the chimney. Or the roof. Or the gutter. He checked the window, which looked out onto the small backyard. Below stood a single-storey lean-to with a slate roof. Martin used it as a shed to store junk.

He touched the sill of the window, an old-fashioned, sliding-sash one with thick layers of white gloss paint. Spongy. Maybe it could be repaired. Probably not. You'd have to dig out all the rot, treat any good wood left and then fill it. The place was listed so any replacement window would have to be in character. Expensive. And it was difficult to double glaze a window like this. Which didn't help with heating bills.

He tried to lift the sash. Stuck. He tried harder and it suddenly shot up. The cords must be broken. He'd have to be careful. When he was a kid they'd lived in an old house with windows like this. Once he'd tried to lift a sash up and it had crashed down onto his fingers. He'd been trapped, screaming his head off with the pain. Eventually his mother had heard him and freed him. His fingers had been ridiculously flattened, like in a cartoon. But not broken. Though the pain had been awful for days afterwards.

He sat down on the only chair in the room, a wooden one covered with paint splashes. Pieces of wallpaper covered the bare floorboards. He'd known that the house was 'in need of some renovation', but he'd not imagined that it could be this bad. The agreement with Lester was that he could stay here rent-free while he carried out the necessary repairs. They'd had to sell the house he'd shared with Julie to pay for her treatment. Without Lester's help he'd have been on the street.

Lester had bought the place for next to nothing on a whim a few years before. From an old man who had died in hospital. Prospective purchasers had been put off by the many repairs it needed.

Martin had put every penny he had into the repairs, but there was still lots to do. And he had no money left for builders. He would have to do it himself. He went through the list in his head: roof, chimney, gutters, downpipes. He'd have to borrow a ladder. Get a roofer to have a look and take his advice without giving him the job. You'd have to use real slates, and maybe the authorities would insist on cast iron rainwater goods.

If the windows needed to be replaced, that would be six. Three at the front and three at the back. Sliding sash windows; they would have to be specially made. He examined the area of wall he'd cleared down to the original plaster—it was coming off in chunks. It would have to be replastered. He could do small areas himself, but not this much. And if the windows were rotting, what about the floorboards? There were signs of rising damp on the ground floor walls. He might need a new damp-proof course. Maybe a new floor and damp-proof membrane. And the outside walls might need repointing.

Basically the whole house needed to be gutted and refurbished from scratch.

He went downstairs and got out the wallet-full of CDs that Lester had given him, and shuffled through. *Music from Big Pink, Loudon Wainwright, Love, Stormcock, Weather Report*. Songs for a funeral playlist needed to be uplifting, not maudlin or full of doom and gloom. Not too obviously happy-clappy, though. Not *Always look on the bright side of life*.

The collection contained a few hard rock and heavy metal CDs: AC/DC, Motorhead. Now that would be inappropriate for a funeral. What he needed was some hippy music from the Seventies.

Those days forty years before, when he'd shared a flat with Lester and John, had been the best days of his life: Listening to Fairport Convention's *Liege and Lief* while tripping; Richard Thompson's guitar setting his whole body vibrating.

He put on *Stormcock*, sat in the armchair with a cup of coffee, and skimmed the file Lester had given him while Roy Harper's guitar gently played in the background. He sang along: 'You can take a horse to water but you cannot make him drink.' It'd been more than thirty years since he'd heard the words but they were still fresh.

A memory: Sitting with Lester and John, listening to Roy Harper and smoking dope. Sun shining through the big window. A dream. Forget about John Hardin. Do some work.

He sorted through the papers. It looked like the Liverpool City Region Strategy to 2020 was based on the 'Visitor Economy'. Investment in culture and heritage: hotels, shops, the city centre. Golf courses.

He spent ten minutes rearranging the file into some semblance of order, then put it down with a feeling of satisfaction at how neat it all looked now. He gazed at the wall. Was this the answer? Liverpool was a city built on its port, on trade. That had all changed with the loss of the empire and then containerisation of the docks. Then the car industry had declined. All that was left was some light industry at Speke, Huyton and Kirkby. Maybe this Visitor Economy idea was the only option.

But wouldn't the jobs created be minimum-wage, zero-hours jobs? He would have to think about it.

The other strand of the strategy emphasised new housing development. The euphemism seemed to be 'improving the mix'. Bring home owners into the city, people who would have jobs, spend money in shops and pay their income and council tax. Yuppies. But you needed good, well-paid jobs to attract yuppies. Sites for modern Silicon-Valley-style industries near to motorway junctions and handy for the airport. He went to the table and unfolded his Ordnance Survey map of Liverpool.

The problem was that the city had been tightly built up within orbital motorways and major roads. Not many brownfield sites left. Unless you created them via demolition. Or used greenspace and parks. He traced his finger along a motorway to where it joined another one.

He started up his computer, went on the council

website and checked the OS map against the Unitary Development Plan on the screen. The motorway corridor was the obvious place. He spent a good five minutes searching the map. Nope. Nothing doing.

A new track started and he sang along: 'I never know what time of day it is, sitting on top of the fire …' This could be one for the list. Intricate guitar. Uplifting. Optimistic.

He checked the online papers and news websites. Nothing about John Hardin.

John's keys and mobile remained in the satchel, which hung off the back of a chair. After the do with the cops he'd nipped back to the office for it, taking a roundabout route just in case anyone was watching. He checked the mobile; its call history had been wiped clean. Why would you do that? He put the keys and mobile in a carrier bag and tied it up. The bedroom had a loose floorboard, perfect for stashing the bag out of reach of prying fingers. And that's where it could stay.

The CD reached its end as he came down the stairs: 'Dead on arrival, where I stand!'

A loud knocking sounded on the door.

CHAPTER FIVE

'I really appreciate what you did for me, Lester,' Martin said.

They sat down at the kitchen table, each with a cup of tea. Lester's frame filled the seat. He put an iPad on the table and thrust his big, beaming face towards Martin.

'That's what friends are for, old boy,' Lester said. 'When you've done a lot of climbing with someone, put your life in their hands, trusted them completely, something develops that's more than friendship. John Hardin was different. When you climbed with him you were just a moving belay. Something to help him achieve his ambitions. Like in that incident in the Alps with Al Hopkins. That didn't surprise me. And as for all that other stuff, that's what friends are for. I still can't understand how they pinned the blame on you. Your boss told me once that you were the best planner he ever had. "If you ask Martin Bennett to do something, he just does it," he said. "So meticulous."' Pause. 'It can't have been easy for you.'

'Well, I really appreciate it.'

After a few moments, Lester said brightly, 'How's the growth strategy going?'

'I'm reading through it. Give me time. I'll come up with some ideas soon.'

'Excellent,' Lester said. 'No pressure. Got the file safely under lock and key?'

Martin nodded.

Lester laughed.

'What about when we were driving into Mold in Al's old van and the brakes failed?' Martin said.

'Open all the doors! As if we were in an aeroplane and the doors were flaps.'

'And those ragged Hellys with his balls hanging out. When we shared the flat in Chester he used to go to the pub in them.'

'Mothers would put their hands over their children's eyes. He died in them.'

'Do you believe the official account?'

'Of course; I was there. He went for a piss on the ledge and didn't clip in like he was supposed to.' A touch of indignation entered Lester's voice. 'We didn't leave him to die. Does Amy ever talk about it?'

'Never.'

'Her mother asked me to help out. Amy was finding it difficult to get an internship after university. She did fantastically well on the green belt job so I gave her the permanent position.' Lester stared into the distance, then smiled. 'We sweated and pissed blood to save that green belt, didn't we?' he said, changing the subject a little too obviously.

'We did.'

'Well, it looks like we're going to lose it now anyway the way things are going.'

Martin frowned. 'It was always under threat, wasn't it?'

'Yeah, well now it's the shortage of housing argument.'

'The answer to that was always to build on the brownfield sites first.'

'But they're now saying that they've developed all the best brownfield sites and that, anyway, no one wants to live in those kinds of areas. They say things have changed. You can't separate town and country now. Green belts are a nineteenth century concept. Now farmers produce a lot more from less land. There's been four million added to the workforce over the last twenty years, and they all want mortgages. Yet the number of houses being built is at an all-time low. Now most people have cars and don't have to live within walking distance of jobs, shops and public transport.'

'I don't know, Lester,' Martin said. 'I appreciate all that, but what about stopping urban sprawl? Without the green belt Liverpool would have joined up with Manchester by now. Just concrete, no countryside.' He paused, trying to remember all the other arguments. 'Look at Woolton village—completely swallowed up by Liverpool, yet everyone still refers to it as the village.'

'Okay,' Lester said brightly. 'We'll have to agree to differ.' He grinned. 'What about that farmer who thought we were after his land and came at us with the shotgun? "Put another leg over that fence, my lad, and I'll give you a barrel of this in your guts. Your pal can have the other one."'

'I shat my pants, mate. I really thought he was going to do it.'

'I did too. You could see it in his eyes. Cold, like a haddock's on a fishmonger's slab. And then he put that notice up.'

'Martin Bennett, Prince of Darkness. Keep out!' Martin laughed. Should he mention the Irish Streets project? No, it would be a waste of time.

'Have a look at this.' Lester switched on the iPad and pushed it towards Martin.

Martin pulled the iPad towards him and read out the title of the You Tube film on the screen, 'John Hardin, Adventure Climber'. He pushed the play button.

The film looked like it was set in the Eighties. John Hardin—long blonde hair, head band, bronzed, muscled—doing pull ups, first with two hands, then one hand. Finally with one finger. Then climbing. Solo. In the sun. America. Rock formations. Badlands? Half a dozen routes that looked impossibly hard, all effortless.

The film finished and Lester laughed. 'The golden boy.'

'Looked like a film star, didn't he?'

'I once looked like that. Well, something like that.' Lester patted his belly. 'Not any longer. So what did your old mucker, John, have to say for himself before he died?'

'Oh, he talked about old times.' Martin paused. 'You know he wasn't my mate.'

'I'd gathered that. Do you still bear a grudge?'

Martin blushed and looked away.

'It's not much fun being a cuckolded husband, Lester,'

he said after a while. 'Realising that your wife wants a more attractive man. That you have been defeated in life's rutting ritual. John laughed in my face. Even when I was chasing him around the kitchen with a breadknife. He might as well have ground my face into the muck with his boot.'

'He did it to lots of people,' Lester said. 'You weren't alone: wives, daughters, mothers, grandmothers, maiden aunts. There's an urban myth about how so many kids in Liverpool look like him.'

Silence.

Lester looked embarrassed. 'Talking of which,' he said at last, 'have you heard Freud's favourite joke?'

'No, but I'm sure you're going to tell me.'

'You'll like it. One fine morning, the Austro-Hungarian Emperor is walking through the streets of Vienna when he meets a man who is his double coming the opposite way. "I say, sir," the emperor blurts out, a grin on his face. "Did your mother ever work at the palace?" "No," says the man, taken aback and puzzled. "But my father did."' Lester looked at Martin for a moment, then turned away when he saw that Martin wasn't laughing.

'And the worst of it,' Martin said after a long silence, 'was that Julie threw herself at him, made a fool of herself. And what did he do? Dumped her like a sack of rubbish by the side of the road. Not that she can see the truth. She blames me.'

'Blames you?' Lester laughed.

'Yeah. I had a sort of an affair with this woman from work. Went out for meals at lunchtime, walks in the

41

woods, that kind of thing. Didn't even consummate it. But someone saw us and told my wife.'

'I liked Julie. I felt sorry for her. She tried to ... didn't she?'

'Commit suicide? She took an overdose, then the tablets they gave her to calm her down turned her loopy. I was blamed. House sold to pay for the treatment. And then I lost my job ...'

Neither man said anything for a while.

Martin broke the silence. 'So was Orwell right?'

'What?'

'Is life just suffering? Look at me. I'm fifty-five, losing my hair, putting on weight. Not exactly an oil painting, am I? I'm not even a badly-executed watercolour.'

'Hah? You're not fat. You're like a stick of spaghetti compared to me! Wait until your widow's peak at the front starts to get on speaking terms with your bald patch at the back. And the distinguished grey bits start joining together so you look like a geriatric badger. That's the time to worry. Look, Martin. I've lost everything: wife, kids, home. Once I was a contender, but what am I now?'

He slurred his words. Had he been drinking? No, too early in the day.

'I'm a bum,' Lester said. 'An alcoholic bum.'

'Nice Marlon Brando impression, Lester.'

They both laughed and took swallows of their tea.

'Yes,' Martin said at last. 'If the police are looking for a suspect then I'm their man.'

'I could challenge you on that. I didn't like him either.'

Martin had once dreamed of jamming John Hardin's

balls in a vice, tightening it up then attacking his dick with a lump hammer. He wasn't proud of this, but it was what Hardin had deserved.

'Some of the things he did were a little uncalled for—' Lester continued.

'Uncalled for?' Martin snapped. 'He was a piece of shit ... and even though he's dead, he's still a piece of shit to me ... destroyed my marriage.'

'That's a bit harsh. Okay, he could be a bit churlish, but—'

'Lester, he was a piece of shit. Spell it: S.H.I.T.'

'Okay, he used to play tricks—'

'Tricks? You mean sadistic practical jokes? Putting big stones in your rucksack. Sitting in the back seat of a car and putting his hands over your eyes while you're driving at seventy miles an hour? And leaving his mate on that climb in the Alps. Leaving him to die.'

'There were different opinions about that. Some said he went for help.'

'He left Hopkins to die.' Martin said. 'And what about that letter he sent to Mountain magazine about you?'

'He accused me of being a cheat. And I thought he was my friend.' Lester stared straight ahead, a strange expression on his face. 'No, if you're a suspect then I would be too.'

'Knowing John there'll be lots of suspects.'

After a long pause, Lester reached for the iPad. 'Hey, look at this. Remember last week when you called me a liar over me beating Seb Coe?'

'I didn't call you a liar ...'

'In so many words. Well, have a gander at this.'

The caption on the You Tube video read *Gateshead 1500 metres, 1980.* The film was slightly blurred and out of focus. Lester often showed Martin videos of past middle-distance races or music videos of Seventies and Eighties bands. This one showed a line of runners setting off. Coe was obvious, with his upright stance and easy running style. All in white. A tall figure in darker shorts and vest tracked him, clumsy compared to Coe, but powerful-looking. Coming into the home straight the camera got a brief close-up of the tracking runner as he began his sprint for the line. For a brief moment it caught the demented expression on his face. This was it. The big chance. Coe fought all the way, but his opponent just got his chest ahead on the line.

'It was a flash in the pan,' Lester said. 'Coe had a virus or something. I finished eighth in the Olympic trials the next month. Never came close to the big time again. But I can say that I once beat Sebastian Coe.' He grinned at Martin. 'I need a slash.'

While Lester was away, Martin checked the browsing history on the iPad. Lester had been on You Tube all the previous morning. There was a gap of about an hour at the time of John Hardin's death.

Martin had his first suspect—apart from himself. But then Martin couldn't be a suspect. He was a witness.

Lester came in and pointed at the chimney breast where a foot wide black stain ran halfway down the wall. 'What's this? Condensation?'

'It's the flashings on next door's chimney. I got a

builder in to put some slates back, and he pointed it out. Said it wouldn't cost that much, but I needed to get the owner's consent.'

'And?'

Martin shrugged. 'He's a recluse. A hermit. I've tried knocking on the door, but he never answers. I know he's in, but he won't answer. I've never even seen him really, only caught glimpses of him. He throws rubbish and empty bottles over the wall. Plays TV from morning to night. *The Karate Kid*, things like that. That's the only sign there's anyone alive in there. Apart from the sound of pissing in the toilet.'

'I thought these old buildings had thick walls.'

'Nah, there's loads of cracks. It's like he's in the same room.'

'Well, keep at it.' Lester said. 'Your kitchen could do with a tidy up, too. I'm sure I saw something moving in that sink, amongst all those dirty dishes in the greasy water. Something alive.'

Martin grinned. *Withnail and I* was Lester's favourite film.

'Did you fork it?' Martin said brightly, referring to a line from the film.

'Okay,' Lester said when they'd both stopped laughing. 'Hardin destroyed your marriage, and he ruined my climbing career. We both hated him and wanted him dead. We'd both be prime suspects.' He stopped and grinned at Martin. 'There's only one thing for it.' He paused.

'And what's that?' Martin said.

'Leave it be. Knowing John, he was probably mixed up in something nasty.'

A wailing started up somewhere, so loud that it startled both of them. The sound came from the other side of the wall facing the chimney breast. It grew louder until they could make out some of the words.

'And I-ee, I-ee, I, will always love you ...'

'What the fuck is that?' Lester said. 'It sounds like a cat being butchered with a rusty knife.'

'It's my lovely next door neighbours on the other side. They play Whitney Houston from dusk till dawn, then dawn till dusk. They're quite young too—students, I think, though they never seem to go to college or anything. All I see of them is an occasional pair of hands sticking out the door to collect a delivery of food or a parcel.'

'Well, I would've thought they could play Adele or Ed Sheeran or some shite like that, something that pretends to have a melody.'

'Right. And I've got a coffin-dodging recluse on the other side who throws rubbish over the wall and watches *The Karate Kid* all day and all night.'

The wail turned into a demented shriek. 'Oh, I-eee I-eee I-eee will always love you...'

'Right.' Lester clapped his hands together. 'A good time to go for the run!'

*

'Look at the state of that,' Lester said as they jogged

through the entrance gates to Woolton Woods and the school came into view. The hall peeked round the edge of a four-storey wing.

'Sixties brutalism at its worst,' Martin said. 'I've often wondered if the architects who built that school were having a joke.'

'Only a joker or an idiot would build an extension to a sandstone grade one listed building in concrete blocks.'

'Ian Nairn would've had a fit, foaming at the mouth. Best to take it easy,' Martin added. 'First time out.'

Lester slowed down, already breathing hard. His purple and black tights and red T-shirt emphasised his ample beer belly. The T-shirt had *Let's Fuck While The Bacon Fries* scrawled across it in large white letters. He loomed over Martin who felt like a child next to his dad.

'Good idea,' Lester said, 'seeing as we're a recovering alcoholic and a coffin-dodger with a dicky heart trying to get fit.'

'You're going to get us arrested as perverts with those tights and that T-shirt,' Martin said, slowing down to match Lester's pace. 'Did you find them in the garage in a box of climbing gear from the Eighties?'

'I did, actually. Anyway, what I say is, when you've got it flaunt it.'

They ran on.

'Are you a bona fide alcoholic?' Martin asked after a period of silence. 'Like you go to the AA meeting and say "My name is Freddy Fuckface and I'm an alcoholic"?'

'That's right. I'm only still in work because I own the firm.'

'But you had a skinful yesterday. I thought once you gave up you gave up for good.'

Lester coughed up a mouthful of phlegm and spat it onto the verge. 'Yeah, but I'll have a dry night tonight. And this run will help.'

'So why did you become an alcoholic?'

Lester laughed. 'How about life is disagreeable at best and intolerable at worst? No, if the truth be told, it's because I like being pissed.'

Martin motioned with his hand, and they turned right along a track through big, old beech trees.

'Must be hundreds of years old, these trees,' Lester said.

'Yeah, they date from when this was an estate, run by the hall. But thousands of years ago this was the site of an Iron Age camp.'

They came out of the trees to a view across Garston and the Mersey to the Clwyd Hills in the distance and paused for a moment, jogging on the spot.

'What a view,' Lester said, red-faced and sweating hard. Martin was hardly breathing. 'When we get fit we'll have to go climbing again. It'd be twenty, no, thirty years, since I last climbed.'

Martin grinned, but he wasn't so sure. Lester was unfit, overweight and an alky. He had a vision of a rescue with a helicopter rattling overhead.

They took a route downhill through the woods. At first they stumbled over roots, and then brambles snagged their legs. At the bottom of the hill they burst out of the trees and sent a flock of gulls on the field wheeling and shrieking into the air and startling a lady walking her golden retriever. The dog jumped back with a snort of alarm, then decided it was a game and chased Lester, jumping up at him.

'Best get him under control, madam,' Lester said.

'It's okay,' she said. 'He doesn't bite.' In her mid-forties, she had a blonde hairstyle that was remarkably similar to her dog's. She stared in amazement at Lester's T-shirt.

'Well, I do!' Lester shouted. He charged towards the woman, roaring loudly.

Startled, she backed off. The dog became even more excited, running in circles and barking loudly. The lady managed to get a hand on the dog's collar. She crouched down and put him on a lead, then looked up. 'Aren't you Lester Adams?' She laughed. 'I didn't recognise you out of your three-piece suit.'

Lester stared at her.

'Come on.' Martin pulled Lester's arm and they continued along the field for a few hundred yards. At the end they turned left up the hill. Lester slowed, breathing hard again.

Martin glanced at him in concern. 'Are you okay?'

'I'm fine.'

At the top of the hill they stopped and both sat down hard on a bench.

'Who was that woman?' Martin asked.

'The blonde one who looked like her dog?'

Martin laughed. 'She did, didn't she? I saw a feller in here recently with a pit bull, and he looked just like it.

Short, fat, bulldog face.'

'Pit bull-face, you mean. That was Jane Trevelyan. Works for Whitaker. Assistant or something. She was at one of the meetings I had with him. Taking notes. Why do you ask? Fancy her?'

'I fancy every woman that's half-presentable at the moment.'

'Tell me about it.'

'Remember that Jasper Carrot sketch from years ago?' Martin said. 'About how they'd done this survey of sexual habits, and they'd found that the average person had sex once a week?'

'It was what the average person said they did rather than what they actually did.'

'Right. And Jasper says, "What I want to know is who's getting my share?"'

'Once a week? Once a month would be Nirvana. Once a year would be realistic.'

Martin nodded. 'Well, I've not had sex for four years.'

'That's sex when someone else is there, right?' Lester beamed. 'I can beat your four years and raise you. I've not had that kind of sex for five years.'

'You're exaggerating now.'

'Not much.'

They sat for a while in silence, both staring at the view—out over woodland to the Mersey and the Clwyd Hills beyond. The park was seemingly deserted, not a person in sight.

'I love coming here,' Martin said. 'Getting out in the fresh air. It's like a bit of wild countryside in the city.'

'Apart from the B&Q and the Morrisons supermarket.' Lester pointed. 'And this.' He kicked a Kentucky Fried Chicken box that was lying on the path in front of them. The box flew apart, sending greasy wrapping paper, chicken bones and chips flying everywhere. Lester gathered the mess together with one foot, pushed it back into the box and put it all in a bin that stood by the seat. He kicked a couple of chips into the grass.

'Little scrotes,' he said. 'No respect for the environment.' He resumed his seat. 'This isn't real countryside, though, is it? These trees ...' He pointed at a giant beech tree about twenty metres away. 'They were planted by the lord of the manor two hundred years ago. They enclosed this park and landscaped it for their own enjoyment and shifted the peasants out. Look at the national parks—the Lake District, Snowdonia and the rest—they were created by sheep farming or, worse, grouse farming. The trouble is all these nature programmes on the BBC make it look as if half the world is a pristine wilderness. But they just go to the best bits. And half of it is filmed in zoos. There's no such thing as a natural wilderness anymore.'

'I know all that,' Martin said. 'But at least this is open space with trees. It's a bit of the countryside in the city.'

'If all this was created two hundred years ago, it could be created anywhere.'

'Why not just let nature take its course? Keep us out of it?'

'There you go again, Martin. You're just a fucking tree-hugging hippy at heart, aren't you? That's not how it works. People have got to have houses to live in, factories

51

and offices to work in. Shops to—you guessed it—shop in. If you don't go along with that the world will just steamroller over you and do it anyway.'

Martin said nothing.

'When I was a kid ...' he said after a while in a voice so quiet that Lester had to move his head closer to hear, '... maybe eleven or twelve—before adolescence, anyway—I used to go out to the countryside by myself. There seemed to be more of it then. I used to roam through woods, over hills, messed about in streams. Lost in my own little world. An escape from the world of adults.'

'Problems at home?'

Martin nodded. 'They were always fighting. Shouting. Doors slamming.'

They sat in silence for maybe five minutes, then stood and walked back towards the village.

When they got within a hundred yards of the entrance gates, Lester suddenly shouted, 'Sprint finish!' He raced off, his feet thumping on the tarmac path.

A couple of walkers jumped back in surprise as he thundered past like an out-of-control buffalo. Amused, Martin went along with it. He could've easily caught Lester, but he strode along in his wake.

At the gates, Lester stumbled the last few feet to a sandstone pillar, grabbed it with both hands, then slowly sank down onto his knees. He vomited hard against the pillar. Martin had to leap back to avoid the splashes.

When Lester finished he turned to Martin, his face as white and unhealthy looking as a block of lard. A strand of spittle hung from the side of his mouth. 'I feel like a pig shat in my head.' He put his tongue out. 'Look at my tongue, it's wearing a yellow sock.' He tried to laugh but only coughed and spluttered.

'This running is too much like hard work, Martin Bennett,' he whispered. 'I think we'll have to stick to climbing.' He swallowed hard and waited a moment. 'And I'll burn you off in that as well.'

*

Jane Trevelyan sat down on the bench and contemplated the view out over the river Mersey bending around in the near distance and over to the Clwyd Hills roller-coasting across the horizon.

The altercation with the two runners had almost set off a panic attack. Luckily, golden retrievers weren't aggressive and took such incidents in their stride. She stroked Bruce and tried to calm down. She'd seen the big runner before somewhere, but she couldn't place him. That stupid T-shirt.

Then she got it. The deep voice. He worked for Development Solutions. What a plonker.

She set off along the path. Bruce pulled on the lead; he could hear the shouts of kids and barking of dogs. She brought him to heel and walked on.

She'd planned the walk for a while, had purchased a book on local history and architecture and was eager to visit some of the places she'd read about.

The view was fantastic. Out over the Mersey to the Clwyd Hills with a vague grey line in the far distance marking the Welsh hills. This was the site of the Iron Age hill fort. What a vantage point. She walked on, checking the map as she went. A green field flanked by trees stretched down to a road, mainly hidden by trees. This side of the Mersey you could see the old airport buildings and the low, light-coloured sheds of a retail park.

She walked along and then down to the road through an avenue of trees. A huge flock of gulls, interspersed with the odd crow, marched slowly over the field, rooting for worms. A tree creeper ran like a mouse up the trunk of a big beech tree.

After a sandstone lodge, she came to a busy road, making Bruce walk to heel, then walked along a narrow path between a cemetery and playing fields. Brightly coloured graffiti covered the stained concrete of the changing rooms—a bizarre sight.

She continued through the gardens of a crematorium and past a large sandstone house, then the high walls of a garden and parkland with ridges left from medieval agriculture. Although the buildings and walls dated from the last couple of centuries, this was obviously a place with some ancient history—the hill fort and these ridges were evidence of that. She walked along to Woolton Road. It felt like being a young student all over again. She checked the book: *Woolton Road adjacent to Clarke Gardens and Allerton Towers is one of the loveliest dual carriageways in any British city. Mature trees and stone cottages have been allowed to remain in the central reservation.*

She certainly didn't feel as if she were in a city. It was more like a rural scene in the south of England. She crossed the road and walked down a bridleway enclosed by sandstone walls and out onto a golf course. The footpath sign pointed across it, but she kept an eye out for stray balls. The path went into trees; Bruce pulled at the lead and tried to follow a scent trail—probably a fox. She cursed under her breath and let Bruce follow a narrow path through the trees. The path led out onto an area of grass which steepened into a slope, but this was the only way round. Bruce clambered over a fallen tree, and she followed on a faint path. The slope steepened again, but she saw no other way to go. She held on to rhododendron saplings as she negotiated the slope.

This was silly. She had to go back. But she found herself sliding down to what looked like a big drop at the bottom. She let the lead go and grabbed hold of a birch sapling, just managing to stop herself. About ten feet down, the slope ended in a vertical rock face, the sandstone luminescent with bright green moss. It must be an old quarry.

This was dangerous. There were no warning signs or fences. If you slipped you would just keep going. The path led to a death trap. She clambered back up the slope. Bruce waited at the top, panting and his tail wagging. She worked her way up and put him back on the lead. Through a gap in the trees she saw a fifty-foot high sandstone obelisk, graced with bright graffiti at the bottom in the same style as the stuff on the changing rooms she'd passed earlier.

She sat on a sandstone block to catch her breath. Bruce sat beside her, panting hard. She stroked his back and felt something on his neck. *Not another one.* Her breathing quickened until she was gasping for air. Sweat poured down the sides of her nose. She could taste the salt.

CHAPTER SIX

They cruised down the Dock Road in Lester's Merc. The Anglican Cathedral up on the rise towered over its surroundings.

Lester nodded upwards. 'Remember when we used to go climbing in the cathedral quarry?'

When Martin lived in the flat with John and Lester, they would train for hours on the sandstone walls of the quarry in the cemetery below the cathedral. Now Martin's legs and back ached after the previous day's run. Could this be a side effect of the pills? He'd have to check it out on the internet. He wasn't looking forward to climbing, but Lester had insisted. Once Lester got going on something, that was it. Now it was getting fit.

'Do I?' said Martin. 'How could you forget the tarts on Gambier Terrace when you got to the top?' When they poked their heads over the top, they often surprised working girls patrolling on the other side of the railings, traipsing around in their thigh-length boots and hot pants. Always polite, they'd share a joke—once even a cigarette. Though some of the alkies and junkies who hung out in the cemetery could get a bit aggressive.

'Come on,' Lester said, a big grin on his face. 'I seem to remember you disappearing once. What were you up to? A quick shag?' He turned back to his driving just in time to avoid a car coming the opposite way.

Martin felt himself blushing. 'That's not my style, Lester, and you know it.'

'And what about the junkies at the bottom with needles hanging out of their arms. Remember that idiot with the shaved head and wild eyes, with the big shoulder bag filled with what was probably knocked-off stuff, shoving us around and asking for money?'

'When I shoved back, he produced a knife,' Martin said. '"No need for that, mate," says I. And he says, "Who's going to stop me?" And I says, "Me and my mate." He laughed and when I looked round you were disappearing up the path. And you were twice the size of me.'

'Come on, Martin,' Lester said. 'I'm a fucker, not a fighter; you know that.'

Martin had soloed to the top of the wall where he sat down with his feet over the edge and watched his potential mugger staring up at him for a few moments before he stumbled off muttering to himself.

'Smoking a joint with John in that cave,' Lester said. 'Great days.'

'And that tunnel going off into the darkness. You were a twat telling us those vampire stories of old Liverpool. I can remember shitting myself when we explored it and you grabbed the back of my neck in the darkness.'

Lester giggled at the memory. 'They go all the way to Edge Hill and down to the docks, you know.'

'What do?' Martin said.

'The tunnels, me old mucker. Liverpool's built on

sandstone. Easy to work.'

'Didn't they incorporate them into the sewerage system and the underground railways?'

'Yep. But you can still follow them for miles. Even as far as the docks. You've got to be careful, though. There are sumps that are about twenty feet deep. A kid drowned down there not long ago. The council closed the tunnels off, but the kids have ripped the fencing down.'

'Isn't that a bit far-fetched? Tunnels going all the way to the docks? Isn't it one of those urban myths?'

'Apparently not. A team of cavers and archaeologists made it to the air vent by the Albert Dock. They needed spades and thigh-length wellies, but they did it.' Lester hammered his hands on the steering wheel. 'I'm looking forward to climbing again!'

'The thing is, you've got to build up gradually,' Martin said. 'You can't not do any climbing for thirty years and expect to pick up where you left off.'

Martin wasn't sure that Lester was listening, but after the run and Lester throwing up he'd insisted that they start at the wall where they could climb in relative safety. The consequences of unleashing an over-eager and overweight Lester onto a natural crag too early on were too dire to contemplate.

'I suppose you're right,' Lester said. They'd now arrived in the heart of the city centre. 'Look at this load of crap,' he muttered, pointing up at the latest skyscraper.

'It's not that bad.' Martin wished Lester would concentrate on his driving.

'Not that bad? It's shite. Look at that new multi-story

car park over there. Looks like one of those monstrosities from the Sixties.'

'You're right there. That is a pile of shite.'

When they neared the climbing wall, Lester laughed and banged the steering wheel. 'Why do they always put these walls in abandoned churches?'

'Simple. High ceilings and cheap rents.'

Luckily, Lester had changed the *Let's Fuck While The Bacon Fries* T-shirt for one from the Cropredy folk festival. The kid on reception insisted that they fill in membership forms.

'Listen, sonny,' Lester said. 'I've been climbing for over forty years. From before you were born.'

'Right, sir. But you'll still have to fill in the form.'

Martin managed to get Lester to shut up and fill in the form.

'He's only doing his job,' Martin said as he led Lester to the almost empty climbing wall. Despite the garishly painted walls and overhangs festooned with brightly coloured plastic holds, it retained something of the atmosphere of a Victorian church.

Two kids who looked about fourteen, each wearing beanie hats and long shorts, nudged each other and stared as Lester took off his T-shirt and tracksuit bottoms to reveal a pink leotard. He put on his hired climbing boots and harness—the largest size they had. Martin had to help him adjust the harness to its last setting to accommodate Lester's belly.

They top roped a few easy routes, then moved on to a harder one.

'Plastic holds, bolts every three foot,' Lester said as he moved remarkably smoothly up a mid-grade route. 'I think I agree with Don Whillans. What did he say? "Climbing walls? Climbing walls? There's no adventure on climbing walls!"'

He reached the top and Martin lowered him off. Martin pulled the rope through and tied in. 'Hang on. Best get the hang of it before you do any leading.'

'Bollocks! Where's your sense of adventure!' Lester finished tying in, then turned and approached the steeper overhanging wall.

Martin quickly attached the belay plate to the rope as Lester set up a route that would've been hard to top rope, never mind lead.

After making the second clip, on the lip of an overhang, Lester paused, panting, 'Just watch that rope!' He lurched up for a hold.

A loud crack exploded around the hall, and Lester dropped like a big stone.

'Fuck!' he yelled.

Martin instinctively took in the rope and crouched down to take the impact. When it came it was much more powerful than he'd expected, and he shot into the wall, turning at the last moment to take the shock on his shoulders.

Pain shot through several parts of his body at once. 'Jesus!' he yelled.

Lester dangled in space a few feet off the ground, slowly revolving, staring at the broken hold in his hand. 'What happened there?'

Martin lowered him to the ground. A starkly etched zig-zag line like the camouflage on a First World War battleship slotted across his vision. He rolled along with a wave of grey nausea, then found himself sprawled on the ground. He lay for a few moments until he'd recovered sufficiently from the stroke to sit up. Lester sat facing him. The kid from reception stood over them.

'That's never happened before,' the kid said. He reached over to take the broken hold from Lester. 'These holds are rated for a hundred kilograms.'

'What's that in English stones and pounds?' Martin asked, rubbing his shoulder.

'About seventeen stone,' the kid said, eyeing Lester's beer belly. 'How do you feel? Come on, sit on the bench over there by the reception desk, and I'll get you a glass of water.'

'I don't feel good.' Lester said. 'Look, my thumbs have gone weird. Oh God, my heart's beating like a fucked clock.'

The kid stared at Lester as if he was daft. Probably too young for *Withnail and I*.

Martin sat next to Lester on the bench. Lester took deep breaths and Martin did the same, but quietly. Lester hadn't seemed to have noticed Martin's 'turn'. Martin would have to get one of those fail-safe belay devices— what was it called? A grigri? If he'd had the turn when Lester was high up and being lowered off it could've been disastrous. And if it happened again he'd have to go back to the hospital. 'Take it easy,' the doctor had said. 'Avoid stress.'

The kid put a glass of water next to Lester and sat down at a computer with his back to them.

'Hey.' Martin stood and looked over the kid's shoulder at a You Tube video about half-way through. 'Isn't that John Hardin?' John, with his long golden hair wafting in the breeze like an advert for hair shampoo, was soloing a steep crack in what looked like Yosemite.

'Yeah,' the kid said. 'His obituary was in the paper this morning. I googled his name. I'd never heard of him. Seems like he was a big shot in the old days. Pretty cool hombre, eh?'

'Obituary?' Martin said.

CHAPTER SEVEN

CRUCIFIXION IN THE PARK!

A picture showing Newsham Park sat below the *Echo* front page headline. Nice and peaceful. Except a youth had been found hanging from a post with the word *GRASS* written on his naked belly. The story used words like 'brutal', 'merciless', 'shocking violence', 'sadistic' and 'sick'. The pictures had been withheld as too horrific to show. A pensioner walking her Jack Russell that morning had been confronted by the victim hanging from a wooden sculpture erected to celebrate Liverpool gaining European City of Culture status. A police spokesman, DI O'Connor, had asked anyone with information about 'this sickening crime' to call Crimestoppers on a given number.

Martin threw the paper away and turned to *The Guardian*. He leafed through the main bit. Nothing of interest. Until the next to last page.

GOLDEN BOY OF BRITISH CLIMBING DIES OF HEART ATTACK

By Reg Perrin, The Guardian Climbing Correspondent

John Hardin, the golden boy of British climbing whose light shone briefly but brightly in the 1980s, has died of a heart attack at the relatively young age of 55. Always controversial—in fact, he seemed to seek out controversy—Hardin was renowned for a series of death-defying solo ascents. "Take nothing with you but your boots, your chalk bag and your balls" was his motto.

Born on a St Helens council estate to working-class parents, Hardin was a supremely gifted technical climber. He burst on the scene in the late Seventies with a number of early ascents of the hardest climbs of the day, usually in the Peak District and North Wales. After quickly reaching the top at a precociously young age, the brash Hardin, with shoulder-length blond hair and pop star looks, commenced a series of solo ascents—with no ropes or protection gear, i.e. fall and you die—that stunned his contemporaries.

Hardin notoriously offered a thousand pounds to anyone who could follow him on a day's soloing. There were no takers.

There was a dark side to his personality, however. He was involved in a notorious incident when his partner, John Hopkins, died in the Alps. The accusation was that Hardin had abandoned his friend to save himself, something that Hardin always denied. And there was the case of Lester Adams, a former climbing partner, who Hardin, in the pages of Mountain *magazine, accused of cheating.*

Nevertheless, Hardin will be remembered for his technical ability and cool head under pressure. He never succumbed to commercialism, though he did set up a guiding and rope access business in the US, which was ultimately unsuccessful.

Recently he worked as an instructor with Snowdonia Guides based in Llanberis. His best known saying still reverberates today: "Climb for the delight, not the reward."

Martin considered the photo accompanying the obituary in *The Guardian*—a striking, stock shot of John soloing in Yosemite. Bare-chested, he wore only a pair of skimpy white shorts and long white socks with his rock boots. A bandana held back his long, blond hair, like a cross between an Apache warrior and a Greek god. After staring at the photo for a few moments, Martin threw the paper to one side. He'd had enough of John buggerlugs Hardin.

He leaned back in his chair and listened. All quiet. No Whitney Houston. Then loud splashing like a hosepipe sending a jet of water into a swimming pool. The old git did it deliberately, aiming the stream where it would be loudest.

He picked up *The Guardian* supplement, leafed through and stopped at an article based on the country's newest garden city in Kent. *Britain's housing crisis: are garden cities the answer?* summarised the history of garden cities—Ebeneezer Howard's vision of affordable houses built at low density with green spaces nearby, and the resulting Letchworth and Welwyn Garden city. Photos showed beautiful cottage-style houses set in avenues of mature trees. Some developer had started to build a modern version in a vast, old quarry with the backing of local councils and the government. The author of the article considered the risk that the development might result in a common or garden housing estate and was just a ruse to get around green belt zoning. The author considered, however, that with tight control and careful design this outcome could be avoided. He pointed to the mistakes made with new towns in the Fifties and Sixties—Kirkby, Cumbernauld, Skelmersdale. Poor design, lack of facilities, remoteness.

Martin used a magic marker to highlight the most important bits, especially the hectarage and the number of houses involved. He printed off a plan of the modern scheme in the quarry, adjusting its size to roughly the same as a standard scale. He opened up his Ordnance Survey map of the Liverpool area and compared it to the plan. It looked reasonable. Now all that was needed was a site.

He sat thinking for a while, then went up to the bedroom and retrieved John's mobile and keys from the hiding place. The mobile needed charging; he found a spare cable and plug and put it on. He shuffled through the CDs Lester had given him, put on *Workingman's Dead* and listened to the CD while the phone charged.

'Come hear Uncle John's Band, by the riverside ...'

Time for a cup of tea. The pedal bin in the kitchen overflowed with rubbish. He pulled out the plastic bag and put in a new one, then tied up the old bag and took it outside to the bins in the alleyway just in from the road.

'For fuck's sake!' he exclaimed. The purple bin hadn't been emptied. Then he remembered; the bin men were on strike. Bin collection had been contracted out. Zero-hour contracts and minimum wage. The workforce wanted full-time contracts and more per hour. Whoever was to blame, the result was a stinking mess. He opened the lid of the bin. A bulging green bag was stuffed inside. His were black. An empty whisky bottle lay on one side. Martin never drank whisky. He looked up. A curtain moved at an upper floor window in the house next door. He left the bag next to the overflowing bin.

The mobile had enough charge now to open the screen. Call history cleared. He checked the contacts. Nothing. Everything cleared. But the phone looked well used.

Why would you do that just before you were murdered? Though presumably you wouldn't know you were going to be murdered. No; John must have cleared his phone for a reason. Martin threw the mobile onto the table. Useless.

What was it Julie had said to him? Best not to hate too much. He had a lot to hate John for, but now he was dead. Martin sat thinking for a long time, then made the decision. Let bygones be bygones. Go to the sod's funeral. He picked up his own phone, rang the Royal and asked to be put through to Accident & Emergency.

'Hello, I'm a relative of John Hardin, who recently passed away. Do you have any information on when the funeral might be?'

He had to wait while they contacted the ward sister.

'Hello?' came a female voice. 'Are you a relative of Mr Hardin? I'm afraid we can't give out information on our patients. I'll put you through to Admin.'

Martin waited patiently for a couple of minutes. Then a male voice.

'Central Admin here. I understand you're making enquiries about a Mr John Hardin. Mr Carter tried to contact a relative but without success. Mr Hardin was cremated this morning.'

Martin thought about this for a few seconds. 'That was quick? Is this Mr Carter a relative?'

'Mr Carter was Mr Hardin's solicitor and the duty solicitor. He followed the standard procedure when the deceased has no contactable relatives and no fixed address.'

'But it just seems so quick.'

'He couldn't find any next of kin, so he arranged for the cremation. Dr Martino signed the death certificate, and the funeral director picked up the body from the mortuary. It's a set procedure.'

'But shouldn't the police be involved? The coroner? Shouldn't a post mortem have been carried out?'

'This death wasn't suspicious. It was the result of a heart attack, so there was no need for a post mortem. Are you are a relative of Mr Hardin's? Could I just take your details for the records?'

Martin put the phone down on him and rang the hospital again. This time he asked to be put through to the Cardiac Unit.

'Hello, I'm trying to contact Dr Martino. I'm a colleague of his.'

'Dr Martino is no longer with us.'

'But I need to contact him urgently.'

'He's gone back to the Philippines.'

Just like that? 'Uhh, do you have a contact number?'

'I'm afraid we can't give out information like that.'

Martin put the phone down and sat for a long time thinking things over. Everything had changed but he couldn't think what to do. His mind was blank. He leaned back in his chair. *Think about something else.*

On the CD player, Gerry Garcia sang, 'One way or another ...'

CHAPTER EIGHT

The Anglican cathedral loomed above him in the gathering dusk, like a mountain emerging from the mist. Beyond shone the lights from the wheel. Martin paused for a moment to take in the view. On the other side of the street, the four-storey facade of Gambier Terrace stood almost as impressive as the cathedral, the wing to the left built first in sandstone in 1837. Then they ran out of money and had to build the right-hand portion in cheaper yellow brick. John Lennon and Stuart Sutcliffe stayed in a flat there in the late Fifties, and in the early Seventies it was a location for *Gumshoe* starring Albert Finney. No tourist minibuses tonight. All quiet. Martin had asked the taxi driver to stop at the end of the terrace so he could walk back—and check that no one was watching the flat.

More listed buildings in Liverpool than Bath, Martin thought with great satisfaction as he walked along the street. The area around the cathedral had changed. The prostitutes of the old days seemed to have moved elsewhere. Parking meters where once you parked for free.

The cathedral quarry was right opposite Gambier Terrace, the cathedral itself rising up on the other side. He walked down into the quarry along a path enclosed by high, vertical, sandstone walls. The cathedral soared overhead. The tomb had been cut into the rock face like a cave. You had to stand on an ancient gravestone to get in, its surface so weathered that you couldn't read the inscription. A rusty chain-link fence had been pulled to one side.

He wore jeans and trainers and, forty years older than the last time he visited, had to make a good heave to get up. The cave was about twenty feet square, the dusty floor strewn with chip papers and turds. He noticed a little black, plastic box on the floor and picked it up: Little Imps. When he was a kid they'd been in tins. Satanist diagrams—five pointed stars seemed to be the commonest—covered the sandstone walls. One message read *Sade lives!* Did this refer to the Marquis or the pop singer? At the back of the cave, a low tunnel led into darkness. They'd never had a light apart from a few matches for the joint so they'd never gone far in.

Something echoed in the distance. Martin switched on his lighter and crept forward, stooping down in the roughly five-foot high tunnel. The noise became clearer. The sound of rushing water. What was it Lester had said? The authorities had incorporated the tunnels into the drainage and sewerage systems. The floor was sandy, sometimes bare sandstone, with an occasional stone or brick and, once or twice, pools of water that he had to edge around, his feet sinking into mud. The walls had occasional stretches of brickwork and, overhead, areas of neat brick vaulting. The air was cool and surprisingly clean. He felt the flow of air on his cheeks, heard the distant clatter of a train.

Several metres in, a pool of water flooded the tunnel. He tested the depth with a foot, but even at the edge the water lapped towards the top of his boot. It would be deeper in the middle, maybe enough to drown someone. Something clattered not far away, the noise quickly became louder. A train. He ran.

The climb up to the cave from the gravestone was easier in reverse. He walked up to Gambier Terrace and drew two keys from his pocket, one for the main door and one for the flat. If John had been a new tenant then maybe the others wouldn't have got to know him. Best to be confident.

Martin flicked on the lights, revealing a bright and cheerful flat: cream painted walls, wooden floors, bare apart from a table, a couple of chairs and a sofa. Standard IKEA stuff. French windows. Bedroom. Double bed. Duvet. Suitcases and bags. Bathroom. Bath full of soaking clothes. Brown water. Small kitchen. Cupboard with a single tin of baked beans. Fridge with a carton of milk well past its sell-by date. One egg.

If John had been murdered, then the cops would be here soon. Martin had to be careful not to leave any prints.

He went back into the bathroom and pulled the plug. The clothes gave off a sour smell when they were disturbed—must have been soaking for a while. The water drained out, leaving a grey ring of scum in the bath.

He ran the water. No hot, just cold. The clothes were all knotted together. He separated and rinsed them as best he could and draped them over the side of the bath. Underpants, socks, a couple of T-shirts.

Why had he done it? He had no idea, except that he felt that if someone died, their dirty linen shouldn't be left festering in a bath of cold water.

He went into the bedroom and looked under the bed: a pile of mags in a sea of crumpled tissues. He pulled the mags out. Most had lost their covers, and they were all well-thumbed and yellowed with age, giving them the air of a pile of mags from the Thirties discovered in an attic. From the hairstyles, they dated from the Eighties, the sort that used to be displayed on the top shelf in newsagents before the internet provided anything anyone could want in terms of porn at the touch of a mouse. One still had a cover: *Saucy Over-60 Moms*. In fact all the models were somewhat past the age of consent. In the corner someone had scribbled *1955* in biro. Why write it on a porn mag? He put the pile back and sat on the edge of the bed, thinking.

Voices in the hallway outside. A key turned in the lock. It grated. Voices again. Scratching noises at the lock.

Martin rushed to the French windows, unlocked them and looked out: fire escape coming down from above and continuing to the ground. He stepped onto it, pulled the floor-length curtains until they were almost together and closed the windows, leaving them open a crack. He took a couple of steps across the fire escape, but his shoes echoed on the metal. He stopped and crept back, trying to control his breathing.

He could see the back of a terrace of houses in the next street. Lights on. Someone washing up in a kitchen. Below the fire escape, a row of large dumpster bins in the backyard. Different colours: green, purple, blue. Extra-large bins to serve all the flats.

Voices in the flat. Harsh and scouse. High-pitched.

'Come on, let's be quick. We need to do the job properly this time. He won't have hidden any of the fucking money or the gear here, that's for sure. But there might be some clues. Look for a mobile, a computer, iPad, letters. Anything like that. If the twat hadn't been so quick legging it down into that quarry we'd have had him. And we'd have made him talk. And why did the cunt have to die so suddenly like that? I could have killed him, I really could.'

Someone grunted, low and heavy, like a large dog clearing its nose after swimming.

For maybe five minutes Martin listened as the pair searched the flat.

'There's fuck all here.' A squeaky voice. 'The cops must have been through the place with a fine-tooth comb. Look, I'll check the bedroom, you check the fire escape.'

Martin braced himself. When the French windows opened he would crash them open on whoever was inside and try and make a run for it.

Nothing happened. Whoever it was, was taking his time.

'Hey! Come and look at this, Gobby!' The squeaky voice came from another room. 'Look what I've found under the bed! His porn stash!'

A few moments, then: 'The dirty bastard. No letters or anything?'

'Nothing, Mick.'

Gobby and Mick.

A mobile rang.

'What? Right! Come on, Gobby, time to go.'

A couple of seconds later, the door slammed shut, followed by the noise of hurried steps on the stairs, and finally the slam of the front door.

Martin sat on the bare metal of the fire escape. He remained there for a few minutes, then got up and made to open the windows and go in again.

Voices. Lower this time. He stepped back, shut the windows and walked carefully down the escape. It was almost dark now. At the bottom the row of bins stood against a wall. Opposite, a door led into a back alley. Bright white light overhead. Voices in the alley. Quite a way away. The coast was clear for now. He opened the top of a big, purple dumpster. Quarter full. He clambered in, trying to ignore the stench. Something under his feet. He leaned down and picked it up: an iPad. He picked a butter wrapper off it. Why put such an expensive piece of kit in a bin? He manoeuvred himself until he half squatted, half knelt with the iPad in his lap. He shut the lid, then fumbled in his pocket until he found his lighter. He flicked it on, then ran a finger over the iPad's screen. Code word? He put in *1955*. Bingo! He checked the recent emails.

Benny Carter, MM, BH, Gayle Hardin, Julie Bennett, the last with photos attached. He flicked one. Debbie.

Julie Bennett, Martin's ex-wife. Debbie, his daughter.

He put the iPad down and rummaged in his pocket for a biro. The lighter had gone out and he had to flick it on again. He wrote names and initials on the back of his hand.

The door to the alley opened, creaking on its hinges.

Martin closed the lighter and put it back in his pocket. He placed the iPad down by his feet, then carefully lifted the lid until he could just see out. A man with a big face stood in the white light, sideways on. A green trilby hat perched on his thatch of white hair. The mouth, under a big white moustache, opened into a grin; the light caught a startling variety of yellow-stained, blackened and gold-filled teeth.

'There they go!' A voice from nearby.

'You chase them, Pemberton!' shouted the man in the trilby. 'I'm too old for this kind of thing,' he added to himself. He leaned against the wall, got out a pack of cigarettes and lit up. After a moment he followed the sound of running feet.

Martin let the lid down without making a sound. Now was the time for a dart. He would have to leave the iPad in case he was pulled.

*

He didn't have enough money in his pockets for a cab back, only enough for the bus fare, so he caught a bus and sat mulling things over while it seemed to follow every back street in Liverpool. He was surprised at how much had changed since he'd last used public transport. Whole rows of shops demolished and bland retail warehouses put up that could be in any city in the country. And row after row of terraced houses gone.

A lady got on the crowded bus and sat next to him. After a few seconds she wrinkled her nose and moved. He'd obviously brought the smell of the bin with him.

Back at home, he stripped off all his clothes and had a shower. Wrapped in a couple of towels, he took a black magic marker and a roll of sellotape and went up to the spare bedroom.

Everything was quiet. No Whitney Houston. No splashing. He squatted down, lifted a piece of wallpaper about three foot square that was hanging down, taped it up and wrote the name *JOHN HARDIN* on the wall as neatly as he could with a black felt-tip. He thought for a moment then added the word *LEADS*. Underneath he wrote:

Benny Carter
MM
BH
Gayle Hardin
Julie Bennett
Debbie Bennett

He examined the list of leads, pausing on each one for a moment. Benny Carter. He'd vaguely heard of him. Wasn't he a solicitor or something? MM? Nothing. BH—the same. Gayle Hardin—John's ex-wife.

Julie Bennett—his own ex-wife. Debbie Bennett—his daughter.

Anger surged through his body. Why would John have Julie and Debbie's email addresses? And pictures of Debbie. Was he some kind of pervert?

He let the wallpaper hang free again.

CHAPTER NINE

The breakfast porridge kept repeating on him, and the heavy vibration and diesel smell of the old taxi didn't help. It took all his willpower to avoid being sick. The notice in his face read *No smoking or eating food in this vehicle,* and the surly driver would definitely not take too kindly to Martin's breakfast being splattered all over the back seat of his cab. Especially at this time in the morning—before the rush hour. The traffic moved along steadily. He had to retrieve that iPad; it was crucial evidence. The taxi turned into Gambier Terrace and had to manoeuvre around a bin lorry emptying the purple bins. The strike was over. The binmen whistled loudly and chattered amongst themselves. They had won. The taxi sat ticking over for a few minutes as Martin considered what to do next. The driver turned with a quizzical look on his face. Martin let out his breath. The iPad was heading for the tip.

'Back to Woolton, mate.'

Now if he could only keep that porridge down.

*

Martin closed the front door of his house and rammed

the bolt home. He went to the back door and did the same. That was one good thing about a two up two down, you only had two doors. Relatively easy to keep intruders out.

He looked in the fridge. Empty. Apart from a plastic bottle of orange juice. God, he could do with a proper drink. He opened the juice, took it into the lounge and flopped onto the sofa.

He finished the juice then took a black felt-tip, a roll of sellotape, his iPad and the phone book and went upstairs. He sorted through the CDs and put *Music from Big Pink* on the player. Soon the first *Tears of Rage* guitar lick was echoing around the room. He sellotaped the strip of wallpaper up, then pulled a desk and chair from their position in an alcove until they faced the wall. He put the laptop on the desk and the rest of the stuff on one side, then sat at the desk and stared at the list on the wall: John Hardin, Benny Carter, MM, BH, Gayle Hardin, Julie and Debbie. Next to John's name at the top he wrote *'Why put an expensive iPad in the bin?'*

The only way to check up on why Julie was on John's contact list would be to go and see her. If she would see him—and answer questions. He checked *Gayle Hardin* in the phone book: 2 Tipperary Gardens. That was in the Irish Streets area. He wrote the address next to the name on the wall. MM? Nothing. The same with BH. What was the guiding company the obituary had said that John worked for in Llanberis? Snowdonia Guides. He wrote this on the wall, then googled it and checked the staff on the web-site. Ben Hammond. BH. He wrote the name next to the initials. Now he was getting somewhere.

Benny Carter. That sounded familiar. The one who'd arranged John's hasty cremation. Wasn't he the lawyer who was involved with the footballers?

Martin hummed along to *We Can Talk About It Now* and googled Benny Carter. He found company details and a lot of articles about Carter's colourful career. He was currently being investigated on charges of money laundering and bank investment fraud, and his firm was on the verge of bankruptcy. Martin closed down the machine and leaned back in the chair. Right. Some dead ends; some leads.

'The investigation starts here,' he murmured. It was risky and foolish. Downright daft. But it had to be done. This room would be the nerve centre, just like in one of those investigations in the TV cop dramas, a place where he could follow leads and consider suspects.

He had two obvious suspects. Lester had been deeply hurt by John, a friend, who had accused him of being a cheat in the climbing press. And there was Amy Hopkins, whose father John had left to die in the Alps. Or so it had been claimed. Things like that were never cut and dried. Could anyone be sure how they would react in such an emergency? If you were frozen. Exhausted. You couldn't blame someone for saving their own skin. Maybe Amy had brooded on it over the years and come to the conclusion that John had been to blame. He wrote the heading *SUSPECTS,* then underneath, *1. Amy* together with *Father—death?* Next he added *2. Lester—article accusing him of being a cheat.*

But there was a snag. How would Amy or Lester have known that John was back in Liverpool after an absence of twenty years? They might have seen him on the street. But then why go to the trouble of murdering him on an escalator with an injection? Martin had only caught a glimpse of the murderer, but as far as he could remember he—or she—seemed to be of medium build. Which the police had confirmed from the CCTV evidence. Bigger than Amy and smaller than Lester.

He could've been mistaken. Or maybe Amy or Lester got someone else to do it. It didn't make sense. He thought for a moment, then added the obvious to the list of suspects: *3. Bad People—Gangsters?* But, presuming John had cheated them of drugs and cash, why would they murder him in a public place and try to make it look like a heart attack?

He checked his phone. Just a text from Lester: *Climbing this afternoon?* He texted back: *Sorry, old bean, not recovered from yesterday*

Lunchtime arrived. He felt tired and hungry. It would be easy to go to the cafe or the chip shop but he had to make a start somewhere on his new, healthier life.

*

He walked into Sainsbury's, deep in thought, and saw someone he recognised at the fruit and veg counter. The man was fatter than Martin remembered and had lost much of his hair. Dressed for the beach—stripy polo shirt, shorts and sandals—he wore large, gold-rimmed spectacles with pink lenses and was concentrating on picking loose mushrooms. The man turned and caught Martin's eye. After a moment of recognition he turned back to his mushrooms. Martin felt a strong urge to go over and grab him and insist that he acknowledge Martin's presence. He'd had this before with ex-work colleagues pretending he didn't exist.

Martin turned on his heel and quickly left the store, almost at a run. He slowed down at the steps, and as he neared the main street, he realised that he was singing *I Shall Be Released* in loud falsetto.

'You sound like one of those old coffin-dodgers who whistle while they shop!' came a gruff voice from behind him. He turned to be see DS Bert Robinson, resplendent in a dark maroon suit, pink shirt and tie and brown brogues. 'Martin!' the copper said. 'Fancy a pint? I've got the day off. No hard feelings, eh?'

Martin opened his mouth to say that it was too early and that he'd not had his lunch, but the next minute he was sitting in The Black Horse in an alcove with Bert, holding a pint. The place was nearly empty. A low buzz of conversation, the sound of horse racing on the telly and the low muzak in the background meant that they could talk without being overheard.

Robinson always bragged and pretended to have a loose tongue about the crime scene and internal police affairs in Liverpool. Martin suspected that a lot of it was bollocks and just a tactic to garner information.

'Listen to that rubbish.' Robinson nodded his head at a speaker on the wall. Someone was softly crooning *Little*

Ol Wine Drinker Me. Dean Martin. Martin didn't mind it himself. It was a bit of a laugh. 'I like rock n' roll,' Robinson said. 'Elvis, Carl Perkins. The Killer.'

'The Killer?'

'Jerry Lee Lewis. Goodness gracious, great balls of fire!' he sang, giving Martin unwanted views of the remarkable range of yellow, blackened and gold-filled teeth in his mouth. He stopped suddenly and looked at Martin. 'I hope you weren't involved in your mate Mr Hardin's activities,' he said, suddenly serious. 'I don't think you were.'

'He wasn't my mate. I fell out with him a long time ago. I hadn't seen him or spoken to him for years. But yesterday I thought I'd let bygones be bygones and go to his funeral. I found out he'd already been cremated. The selfish bastard.'

'Ah, so you know about that, the cremation?'

'Yeah. It was done in a hurry.'

'I'll say. We were having second thoughts about it, and we were going to refer it to the coroner, just in case there had been any funny business. But Benny Carter, the solicitor who arranged it, said that the duty doctor had signed it off.'

'And that doctor's fucked off back to the Philippines. Bit of a coincidence, that.'

'Right. But if the body's gone, it's gone. Nothing we can do. And the CCTV tape's gone missing. There ought to be an inquiry, but I was overruled. Without willingness to act from above, I can't take it any further.'

They both gazed at their drinks in silence.

'If John was involved with bad people in something illegal,' Martin said, 'maybe local gangsters ... that Chuckie Chipchase ...'

'He's still in jail. You helped put him there, remember?'

'Yeah. The CCTV man on the night shift saw strange goings-on at a warehouse on the industrial estate. He clocked all the suspicious activity, rang the police with the registrations of the vehicles and then rang the manager—me. It was great watching you raid the place on the cameras. Just like the Sweeney. Did you tell them they were nicked?'

'Damn right I did. One car turned out to be Chuckie's limo with Chuckie himself inside. You should've seen his face when I told him he was nicked. The ingots on the lorry were filled with the largest amount of cocaine ever busted in Britain. Worth millions. A far cry to how it was when I started off. When it was robbing from the docks.' He tapped the packet of fags and the lighter on the table. 'These things. Spirits. A bit of safe-cracking. Porn. And then drugs. By the Eighties it'd all built up into an empire under Chuckie. Laundered into property development by Wacker Hughes.'

'The Banker?'

'That's him. Lived in Woolton. Quiet. Middle class. Not involved in any violence. Just did the paperwork. But then everything went wrong. After the ingot bust, Chuckie and the entire leadership of the gang were grassed up on a load of other activities—mainly in Europe—and jailed.'

'Wasn't the informer some feller from the North East?'

'Roscoe Scalby. Died in suspicious circumstances in a motor accident in Greece. Trouble is, he robbed money from the suppliers in Mexico and at the same time got paid for informing. Playing home and away. Gambled the lot down the drain before he died. But poor old Wacker was left holding the can. The Mexicans shot him and stitched his face to a football.'

'Ugh! I remember that. It was like something out of a Joe Nesbo novel.'

'Sick. Too much blood and gore in crime novels these days.'

'Too right.' Martin sat back in his seat.

'Anyhow,' Robinson said, serious again. 'Chuckie served most of his time in a Dutch jail—it was safer to keep him there rather than somewhere in mainland UK where he might have busted out. This Jimmy Hughes had to take over the operation while everyone was inside. Hughes is Wacker's nephew. Now that their rivals, the Masons, have gone legit, Hughes is the top dog. Works with his'—Robinson looked around. The sound of the commentator getting excited at the finish of a horse race on the telly meant that no one could listen in—'bent solicitor, Benny Carter.'

'The Masons. Wasn't it Kenny Mason who drowned trying to bring drugs into Cornwall on a rubber boat?'

'That's the one. His partner, Alison, has gone legit. No stomach for the fight.'

'Benny Carter?' Martin said. 'Isn't he the solicitor who organised the cremation, and isn't he the one who represents the pop stars and the footballers?'

'The very same one. He's being investigated at the moment over his involvement in a bank investment fraud …'

'Bank investment fraud?'

'It's a scam. They get punters to invest in dodgy stocks with glossy brochures and promises of saving tax. The problem for them is that the government is cracking down on all that kind of stuff. It's all gone belly up, and Carter's under investigation. Likely to be struck off as a solicitor. The man's desperate. He works for some bad boys who own a front company that has property all over the region. All legit. The NCA have tried to follow it back to the dirty money on the street, but Wacker was too clever.'

He paused. 'The latest word,' he continued, 'is that they've bought land all over Merseyside in the green belt. At agricultural value—growing carrots. Paid buttons. Once it gets redesignated to shopping, housing or whatever, they'll make millions. No, billions. They have links to the politicians and the mayor.' He grinned. 'Allegedly.' He narrowed his eyes. 'Weren't you involved in some sort of green belt scam?'

Martin looked away.

'Okay,' Robinson said. 'You don't want to talk about it.'

'So where does John Hardin fit into this?' Martin said at last.

'He doesn't. He was just a mule for the drugs side of the operation, importing from Dublin through Holyhead to Liverpool. Irish gangsters supply the merchandise. Bad people. Seems like Hardin was involved in adulterating the drugs. Blending them with foreign agents to make them go further. Caused a number of deaths in this city alone.'

'Is that what you were referring to when you said John was involved in a dirty racket?'

'That's right. Here, look at this.' Robinson got out a mobile phone, pushed a couple of buttons and handed it over. 'Have a look at that.'

The image showed the genital area of a man. The penis was a weird mix of colours—the swollen scrotum mainly black but with some purple.

'They mix the crack cocaine with Levasimole,' Robinson said. 'It's a worming drug used mainly by vets …'

'Worming drug?'

'Yeah.' Robinson laughed. 'Strange as it may seem, it has properties that are similar to cocaine. It increases the effect. Unfortunately, it also reduces the numbers of white blood cells and suppresses the immune system. The victim basically rots to death. Eating away your wedding tackle is just one of the symptoms. We've had more than twenty cases recently. They all died horrible deaths.'

Martin took the phone and gazed at the image.

'And hey presto,' Robinson said. 'It's not a new thing, actually. Any drug can be watered or cut down. Antibiotics in the third world, for instance. Not so good if you're a peasant with a gangrenous arm. Just after the war it was penicillin. Not so good if you're a kid with meningitis.'

Martin realised that he was staring at the copper.

'Anyway,' Robinson continued. 'This last consignment

that went missing was a big one. Seems Hardin stole the drugs and the money. Which, in this business, would generally earn you a one way trip out over the Irish Sea in a helicopter—water-wings not included. Bit of a coincidence that he just died like he did. Hughes wants the drugs and the money back. And he's lost face with his suppliers. That's important if you're an up-and-coming gangster.

'The word is they're moving out of drugs and violence. Diversifying. See that bottle of whisky hanging up behind the bar?' He pointed. 'That's not Johnny Walker. It's a spirit produced in a factory somewhere then blended so it looks and tastes something like it. Costs a couple of quid a bottle to produce, if that, and the landlord buys it for ten, then sells it in shots and makes double that. Big money. Same with ciggies. Meat pies. Frozen meals. Not beef like it says on the packet. It's mainly horses.'

'So why are you telling me all this?' Martin said. A copper wouldn't usually discuss cases. How much of this was bollocks? Martin was clearly being used, but for what?

'I've been trying to get retirement for five years. I've had enough. They used to let you go at fifty. You got a full pension and a nice lump sum, and you walked into a job as a security consultant. They say they can't manage without me.'

He laughed before continuing. 'So I might as well become a trouble-maker. I've had enough of the internal problems we've got.' He held up a hand as Martin opened his mouth. 'Can't go into detail about that.'

'Ever heard of a couple of characters called Gobby and Mick?'

Robinson held Martin's gaze for a few seconds. 'How do you know those two?' he said.

'I've seen them around. This Mick character has a high-pitched voice and a foul mouth.'

'Hah! That'll be Mick Malone. He's got the biggest and the dirtiest gob in Liverpool. I've often had an urge to get a bar of soap and wash his mouth out. He's always in that pub at the top of Quarry Street—The Old Police Station—for the Liverpool matches when they're on the telly. Just follow the sound of loud swearing when the opposition scores a goal. He's got a spiky Rod Stewart hairstyle, fashionable twenty years ago. He'll likely be with his mate Gobby Gilbert, so-called because he never says fuck all. Just grunts. Six foot two, eyes of blue. That's across as well as up.'

'Sounds charming,' Martin said. Mick Malone; that must be MM. And Gobby must've been the second of the two at Hardin's flat. 'I might go up to that alehouse just to have a look at them.'

'I'd keep out of it, Martin, if I were you. It's too risky. Did you see that story in the *Echo*? The lad who was crucified in Newsham Park? The grass?'

'I saw that. Nasty.'

'Malone did that. No proof, but it was him. Just pass any information back to me.'

*

Back at the house, Martin went straight up to his command centre, taped up the sheet of wallpaper, sat down at the desk and scanned the wall, felt tip in hand.

He got up the Development Solutions diary on the computer. There had been a meeting on the morning of John's death to discuss the Irish streets. Both Amy and Lester had attended. A cast iron alibi for both. He realised that it was a waste of time checking up on Lester and Amy when it was obvious that it couldn't have been them. Amy was about five-foot tall while Lester was six foot two. Neither could be called average.

He crossed *Amy Hopkins* and *Lester Adams* off the list of suspects and added *Liverpool gangsters* and *Mick Malone*. Then *Irish gangsters*—no names as yet, two leads to follow up. The only trouble was exactly that. Trouble. It would be risky.

'Hah so!' A scream came from the other side of the wall. 'Thunk!' The sound of someone deep in a forest splitting a log with an axe.

'Thunk! Thunk! Thunk, thunk, thunk!'

The Karate Kid. It stopped as abruptly as it had started. A door slammed. Thank god; some peace.

He stood and walked over to the window just in time to see a bottle come sailing over the wall. It clattered across the concrete backyard and came to a halt in clear view. An empty litre bottle of Johnny Walker. How it didn't smash was a miracle.

CHAPTER TEN

James Whitaker had been staring at the view for ten minutes. Thinking about difficult staff. Balloonheads. In the private sector you could just sack them. But that wasn't possible in the fucking public sector. Particularly if you were the mayor. He sighed.

The Wirral skyline was fairly nondescript—blocks of flats and factories. Nearer to hand the waters of an incoming tide on the Mersey roiled and boiled in the foreground with the Liver buildings and the wheel off to one side, and the rolling edge of the Clwyd Hills in the distance.

He turned to stare at the painting on the wall. As high as a man, it showed a pillar of the Liverpool establishment from two centuries ago. He'd built the town hall and several monuments around the city. He looked surprisingly modern—if you took away the silly wig and put him in a suit he wouldn't merit a second glance on the street outside. He certainly looked confident about the future. Not apologetic about anything. And he'd been a slave-trader. Most of his family's money had come from compensation when slavery was abolished. The key thing was not to feel guilty about anything you did. If it had to be done, it had to be done.

James Whitaker had fought long and hard for the powers he had now—and for control of the Liverpool city region. But there was always a downside to any success. Total control of planning had seemed like such a good idea. Great when things went well and you could claim responsibility for successes. But not so good when you got blamed for stuff like failing to find a new use for a stupid bombed-out church. It would all seem so simple to an outsider if you didn't know how things really worked. Like that spin doctor at the last meeting.

'Housing,' he'd said. 'That's what's going to win seats in the next election. Just build lots of houses and promise to build lots more.'

It sounded easy, but it wasn't when you had to deal with planning, green belts, central government and all that crap. Not to mention the balloonheads who hugged the trees that inevitably had to come down.

And when it came to staff, having direct control sounded great, but then you had to do just that—control them.

He searched for his MBA dissertation, got it up on the screen, then read through the mission statement for the Merseyside Regeneration Agency:

We will work with the community to regenerate Merseyside. We are committed to excellence and total quality.

He'd spent long hours on that, long evenings late at night at home, long away days with the board. He flicked through the dissertation. Long quotes from Druckers and Peters. In fact the title of the dissertation was *The Need for Empowerment in the Workplace*. And he stood by every word. You had to respect your staff. They were assets, not liabilities. You empowered them but made sure they were always guided by centralised values. In this case, quality and excellence.

But what about difficult people? He googled it and came up with a list. Was Jane Trevelyan a *Martyr?* An *Absentee?* An *Eccentric?* His executive support officer was certainly *Quarrelsome*, and *Temperamental*. But nothing really fitted. Basically she was a Bleeding Heart Liberal who'd gone native and wouldn't obey orders. Just like Carter, this bastard lawyer, who was giving him so much jip. He lifted the phone.

'Cath, could you spare a moment?'

Cath Benson, his head of HR, came in and sat down—short black hair, well-cut; neat, blue suit; flat-soled shoes—a paragon of primness and properness. He always had a strong urge to put a question to her: 'Do you spit or swallow?' But no. She was a feisty feminist, still under the control of the council she came from and a personal friend of Trevelyan. He would have to be careful.

'So what's the problem?' She held a pad and pen ready to take notes. Everything documented. First rule of HR.

She waved away his offer of coffee. He poured himself one. 'It's not a problem really. Just a little staffing difficulty.'

'Go on.'

'It's Jane. She's proving difficult.'

Cath looked at him for a moment. 'She's not been in the job long,' she said. 'She needs to settle in. This is a whole new area for everyone. The mayor having direct responsibility for staff. The last thing we want is for any inkling of this to get out.' She made a note. 'So what exactly is the problem?' Her pen was poised.

He laughed. 'She won't obey orders.'

'I thought you were against that sort of thing: hierarchical management. What won't she obey you on?'

'Everything. The Irish streets. The bombed-out church. The green belt. The economic strategy. You name it.'

'Can't you discuss it? Come to an agreement? Those kinds of issues always have two sides to them. Maybe it's healthy that she disagrees with you. You wouldn't want a yes man ... yes woman, would you?' She smiled. Sweet reasonableness.

He sighed. 'They're all issues that have been debated to death. We've made a decision on them. If I did a U-turn I'd look weak ...'

She made a note and underlined it, her pen catching on the paper. 'So what do you want to do?'

'Give her a warning. A slap on the wrist. A shot across the bows.' He sipped his coffee.

'We're talking about a senior officer of an agency responsible for one of the country's great cities, not a disobedient schoolgirl. She's in her fifties.' She regarded him with narrowed eyes. 'Are you sure there's nothing else?'

'What do you mean?' He felt his face reddening and knew what the bitch was getting at.

'Nothing.' She stood. 'I'm afraid I disagree with you, James. I'll put a note in my diary. In my opinion, you should discuss it with her. I'll sit in and take notes if you like. Think about it.'

After she'd gone, he sat thinking, waiting for the anger to subside. Only it wouldn't. All sisters together. Balloonheads! He smashed the empty coffee cup onto the desk. A shard whizzed into the air and landed on the carpet. He checked his watch. Only fifteen minutes in which to calm down.

*

Jimmy Hughes changed a figure and pressed *Return*. Although he was a chartered surveyor by profession and must have done it thousands of times, he still loved that magical moment when you pressed the return button, the figures whirred and the spreadsheet changed.

Things weren't going well for Mersey Estates. Sales not moving. Rentals down. Cash flow slowing to a trickle. It was the recession. Loose cannons. Headaches.

He'd parked up behind the new library: a swish-looking place. Must have cost a few bob. He only hoped that it wouldn't be closed by the cuts. Now that would be daft. He'd arrived early, so he sat in the car for a few minutes, checking the spreadsheets on his laptop.

He flicked through the dog-eared draft of a business plan. This was the hard bit. The written stuff. He'd put off going to the bank as long as possible, but now there was no alternative.

The business itself was pretty straightforward. The

main outgoing was wages. Then there were overheads, expenses, bad debts, maintenance. Set against incomes from fees, sales, rents. An admin assistant kept the books day-to-day—finalised for the annual audit by a financial consultant. She had no idea where the money had come from originally to get things going and buy the land and property. Now it was a legitimate business. All tax and VAT paid in full and on time and the dividends paid to the owners. But that was the problem: ownership. As Chief Executive Officer, he owned ten percent. But the remaining ninety percent were silent investors. Would the bank want details? If they did he'd have to withdraw the application.

He thought he'd done a nice resume of the company's history—the original forays into construction and security, the profits fed into property for rent and sale both residential and commercial. Straightforward. He'd written everything down so it wouldn't be lost. Absent-mindedness was one of his weaknesses.

He leaned back in the seat, the plan on his lap. The problem was this SWOT analysis. Strengths, weaknesses, opportunities, threats. The strengths were good: a USP of a quality, reliable service; a wide portfolio; extensive experience; no borrowings up to now. The main weakness was being subject to the business cycle. In a recession, property was always the first sector to suffer: rentals down; sales not moving; cash flow down to a trickle; too much land bought at agricultural value for which you couldn't get planning permission. It was like a mantra, repeated throughout the document.

He reached for a file from the back seat and leafed through the OS plan on which the sites were marked. Fields leased out to local farmers for growing potatoes, carrots, turnips. A lot of them weren't even used for crops—they were set aside under EU rules. There was a great site right by the motorway, more than a hundred acres, except it was a waste tip. No one was going to develop that.

Then there were the white elephants, the biggest of which was the ex-football pools building built in the Sixties: thirty thousand square feet, two floors, steel frame and concrete panels. A good earner if you could let it. But it was a nightmare. Everything was wrong. Services, fire control, parking, size of the potential units. He'd tried everything. He'd had plans drawn up to convert it to offices, light industrial units, even flats, but gardens and car parking couldn't be fitted in. Nothing worked.

Apart from the white elephants, there were many opportunities, of course: a growing student population; same for young professionals; business start-ups; more growing businesses. What the plan needed was a big project that would take advantage of these opportunities.

Now what could he put under threats? He could hardly tell the truth, could he? The recent disastrous publicity. A loose cannon not under his control. A knobhead on the loose who might bring the whole tottering structure down. Chuckie would've sorted it. Two shots in the back of the head, the second to make sure.

Jimmy groaned and thumped a fist into the steering wheel. That wasn't an option for him. You could hardly put that in a business plan, could you? Main threat: mindless knobhead. Solution? Two shots in the back of the head.

He threw the plan onto the passenger seat and walked over to the pub, which had been converted to a Wetherspoons since the last time he'd been there. Though fairly busy, there were plenty of quiet places to sit. The low, piped music would drown out their conversation. He bought a pint of Bombardier and, as he turned from the bar, Harry Bowman walked in, limping on a stick. Heavy grey overcoat, shiny shoes, cap on his head. Big grey muzzy. Jimmy was surprised by how old Harry looked, though he was still a big feller.

'A'right, Jimmy lad,' Harry said. 'Fancy the Bombardier? I'll have the same. It's a good pint in here. Let's find a quiet place where we can have a nice chat.'

Once they were sitting in an alcove well away from any other customers, Harry slapped the table. 'So how's it going?'

'Not so well. I don't want to sound like a whinger, Harry, but it's all getting on top of me.'

'Go on,' Harry said. He took a swallow of beer, put the glass down and leaned back in his seat. 'Get it off your chest, lad.'

Jimmy thought. He couldn't tell Harry about the difficulties at home: the lad who wouldn't work; the daughter being bullied at school; the wife who'd withdrawn from him, who, when he put his hands on her, her arm went rigid, as if something disgusting had touched her. He would sound like a whinger.

'The thing is, Harry,' Jimmy said, 'when I agreed to help out, I made a point of saying that I didn't want to be involved in anything rough or illegal. As far as I'm concerned that is all in the past, and this is a business now like any other. When my uncle was murdered that should've been the end of it.'

Harry had given him the only surviving copy of his uncle's memory stick with the details of the setup. Jimmy had committed the important bits to memory, then thrown the stick onto a red-hot coal fire and watched as it bubbled, hissed, then exploded and shrivelled to nothing. He couldn't let it lie around where he might forget about it.

'It should've been, kid. I'm afraid your uncle was a sacrificial lamb. It was terrible what happened to him, but it should've put an end to it all. And, to be honest, it was a good opportunity for you, Jimmy.'

'Okay, I admit this was a godsend to me. I was on the dole. Almost got a criminal record. Not much fun being a professional man when you might be thrown out of the institute. But I'm a surveyor, not a thug. And Micky has still got his fingers in the shit.'

'Micky Malone? He's a gobshite if ever there was one. God help you if you're relying on him.'

'He's not a gobshite, he's a cunt. He doesn't respect me. I can't control him. Did you see the front page of the *Echo* the other night? The feller crucified in the park?'

'What? The poor lad nailed up on the Merseyside Rising sculpture? Was Micky behind that?'

'Yeh. The latest caper was when this courier was

robbed of the money and the drugs. A transaction I knew nothing about. And then this character goes and dies of a heart attack. Except I suspect someone gave him a helping hand. So the fellers over the water will be pissed off.'

'I don't like the sound of that.'

'It gets worse. This call centre that was supposed to be the big saviour, well, they clawed back a load of the grant. We're skint again. We need to build houses, that's where the money is these days. But there's no land.'

'There's plenty of land. Just go down any main road in Liverpool.'

'Yeah, but it's not in the right place to attract punters, is it? The type of people who are going to pay a mortgage. Where their children can go to nice schools, with nice parks on the doorstep. Where you can go to the corner shop for a loaf of bread and a pint of milk without being mugged. The corpy aren't building council houses any more. There's a bit of building done by housing associations, but not much. We've got this proposal to redevelop this area by the city centre …'

'The Irish Streets? Killarney Terrace, Galway Grove?'

'Yeah. But it's held up by little old grannies manning the barricades on the front page of the *Echo* every night. In the old days they would've just cleared them out, but not now.'

'They're nice houses, them, why can't you do them up?'

'They'd go a bomb in London, but here? Too close to the scallies. We've got a load of land on the edge of the city, but it's agricultural land. There's not much money in carrots and turnips.'

'The thing about land like that, Jimmy lad, is it's all in the planning.'

'Ah, well, it's in the green belt.'

'Green belt? What's that when it's at home?'

'It's protecting the countryside from being built over. Nothing wrong with that ...'

'You know, when I was a lad ...' Harry's eyes took on a faraway look. 'This whole area was fields. That road outside was a lane down which they brought the cows in for milking.'

'Very nice, Harry, but you've got to have progress, otherwise we'd all still be yokels digging in the mud for carrots and turnips, wouldn't we?'

'Anyhow!' Harry slapped the table. 'Get the planning changed from agricultural and you'll rake in the dosh. It was done before, wasn't it? That retail centre. I don't know exactly what happened, but Chuckie and Wacker got the planning changed. Benny Carter knows all about that.'

'I'm onto it. But there's resistance in certain quarters. And Benny Carter's another loose cannon. He's got involved in all sorts of dodgy deals. He's up before the Board of Solicitors soon. He could well be struck off. I've got the feeling he's got an escape route planned to some Caribbean island somewhere before the plods feel his collar. Leaving us in the shit.'

'It was a lot simpler in the old days when we started all this off, Jimmy lad.' Harry had the faraway look in his eyes again. 'Robbing post offices, hijacking lorryloads of spirits off the docks, a bit of safe-cracking. They were great days, them, best days of me life. You had to have skills, you know. Cracking a safe isn't easy. You need to know about combinations, metals, alloys, chemistry. It was a science. Now it's just beating people up or shooting them. Stitching a bloke's face onto a football.' He stopped and watched Jimmy. 'Sorry, Jimmy,' he said. 'I shouldn't have said that. Not after what happened to your uncle.'

'That's okay, Harry.'

'It all kicked off in the war, see. I was born in 1939, and I can remember the sound of those Fokkers overhead. Wuh ...wuh. Wuh ...wuh. There were loads of bombed-out buildings, blackouts, the scuffers over-stretched, Yanks with ciggies, nylons, wads of cash. The lads used to get girls to lure them into a dark alley, then cosh them and rob their stuff. And the docks were packed with stuff: ciggies, whisky, you name it. They used to hop down into the tunnels to escape from the scuffers and hide the stuff.'

'Tunnels?'

'Yeah. They used to go from Edge Hill to by the cathedral and down to the docks. They built them in the Napoleonic wars, and then they were taken over and extended by the underground railways and sewers. We used them in the Fifties. There were all these gangs: the Peanut gang—they used to split open sacks of peanuts on the docks and hand them out to the kids; the Little Gangsters—they would break into cars and go joy-riding; Bomber Command—they used to drop bricks on cars from pedestrian bridges, just for the fun of it; the

Forty Thieves—they would pack into a shop, all forty of them, and rob all the stuff. When I joined a gang in the mid-Fifties it was the Teddy Boys. I had this fantastic tailor-made suit with velvet lapels. Me ma had a few bob then and she paid for it. Proper gear it was. And big beetle-crusher shoes. We used to hang out in the dance halls and at the fairs. It was just fighting at first, before the robbing.'

Harry sighed and slapped a hand on the table. 'The thing is,' he said, 'I can't be doing with all this drugs and guns and that. And as for all this financial stuff and money laundering, I'm not into that kind of stuff. Never used a computer and proud of it, that's me.'

'But you're the only ...' Jimmy's voice trailed off.

'The only one left? You're right there. Chuckie and the rest of the gang are in jail, and your poor old uncle's dead. But there're still a few people who depend on that cheque in their bank account every month. And don't forget that Chuckie and the rest will get out one day, and they'll be wanting nice cosy pensions after what they've been through.'

He turned to face Jimmy. 'We need people like you now to make the most of our investments, not thugs like Micky Malone. I'd like to help, Jimmy, but look at me; I'm a seventy-five-year-old coffin dodger with a bad hip and a dicky heart. Could you imagine anyone being scared of me now?' He finished his pint. 'You're doing a good job, son. The best advice I can give you, Jimmy lad, is get yourself out of the violence and drugs and sort out the planning on those carrot fields.'

'You know what? I think you're right, Harry. You know I'm not the violent type. But if I needed some artillery, where could I get it?'

Harry thought. 'It's a while since I was directly involved in anything like that, Jimmy.' He thought again. 'There was a consignment that was paid for but never collected. It was in one of those lock-ups in West Derby.'

'The ones in Crimea Road, behind the old Pools building?'

'That's it.'

'That's one of ours. I've not been down there for years. We were hanging on to them— hoping to include them in a bigger site. It never came off. Not been maintained for years. Which one?'

'The one at the end, the one with the double doors.'

CHAPTER ELEVEN

'Well, I think we can agree on one thing,' Gayle said when Martin had finished. 'We both hated John Hardin, bless his little cotton socks.'

Gayle Hardin grinned at Martin and laughed, then sipped her coffee. Her blonde hair, cut fashionably short, emphasised her good looks. The tight slacks and black top made the most of her figure too. Martin looked away from the golden skin on an exposed shoulder.

She certainly didn't seem put out by the news of John's death. She had a motive: she'd been abandoned. But would she care enough to murder him? He couldn't see it.

He shrugged. 'I know; I've got more reason to hate him than anyone with all his shagging around.'

Her eyes widened.

'It's okay,' he said. 'I know he did it with Julie.'

'I don't think I despise anyone,' she said, holding his stare, 'as much as I despise John.' For a moment her face set in a mask of hatred, then it eased, and she smiled. 'How's Debbie?'

'Fine.' He looked away, unable to keep eye contact. 'But if you hated him that much, why was your phone number on the contact list on his mobile?'

She sighed. 'He kept phoning up and threatening me. Left nasty messages on Twitter and Facebook. I reported it to the police as harassment, but they didn't do anything.'

'But he was murdered on a hospital escalator. Something should be done about it.'

'Have you told the police?'

'He was injected with something that must have caused the heart attack. It was very quick and hard to spot, but I saw it. The police picked me up and interviewed me. Seems like John was up to no good—drugs, apparently—but they believed it was a heart attack.'

'That doesn't surprise me.' Their gazes met. 'And how are you?' she said eventually. 'In yourself?'

'Not too good. I've had a stroke. I need to take things easy.'

'So you get involved in murder and mayhem. Still working for Lester?'

'Yep. He helped me out when I most needed it.'

'So what happened with that? I heard rumours. It was all over South Lancashire Council. Weren't you sacked?'

'How did you know that?' Martin asked. 'Oh, I remember now; you worked for the same authority for a while, didn't you?'

'Admin. Leisure department. Lost my job a few years ago. Cost-cutting exercise. Anyway, I don't want to talk about that.' She looked down. 'Tell me what happened.'

Martin didn't answer for a long time.

'You know the Interchange Centre?' he said at last.

'Of course.' She looked up. 'IKEA. Marks and Sparks.

Everyone goes there.'

'Exactly. That's why the city centre is in trouble. Anyway, it was the best development site in the area: motorway junction, flat, well-drained, everything. Except it was in the green belt. Lester's firm was commissioned to do a study. I was the council's project officer. We were sworn to secrecy. The site was being considered by a property company who were about to buy it for agricultural value. If it got designated for retail development, it would be worth millions. That's apart from the rents and everything. Big money.'

'And ...'

'The findings of the study were leaked. The property company quickly bought the land at agricultural value and made a killing. Everyone blamed me. I reckon it was this councillor who had links to the company, but they blamed me. Sacked. It was all pushed under the carpet. My career was ended and I lost my pension. Destroyed my marriage.'

'Couldn't you have gone to the police?'

'I did. Police. Union. MP. Everyone apart from the queen and the pope. No one would help. They all assumed I must be guilty. I was ruined. Until Lester offered me a job.'

'A knight in shining armour?'

'That's right. His firm was going through a bad patch, but he took me on. Backroom boy. Lester handles the high-profile jobs and the media while I do the research and strategy stuff. I haven't even got a paragraph and mugshot under the people bit on the website.'

'So let me get this right: these property people earn millions and you get the sack?'

'That's about it.'

'Wow.' She sipped her drink. 'None of that surprises me with this capitalist system we've got. Bankers earn millions in bonuses, and now they're polluting the water with this fracking business and earning billions. And if I earn a few bob they want to tax it and spend the proceeds on invading some country in the Middle East. Everyone's got their nose in the trough. They're even trying to demolish this house,' she waved her arm at the room, 'and the rest of the houses in this area so they can build yuppie houses. There's a meeting tonight where the mayor's going to present his latest proposals. Lying bastard. The system's corrupt. And the mayor's corrupt.' She challenged him with a look. 'Your firm's involved, isn't it?'

'We are. We do project work for the mayor's office. But that one's not my direct responsibility.' He managed to keep a straight face while telling the half-truth. 'Someone else is the project manager.'

'Yes, but you could find out who's behind it, couldn't you? Who's got their snouts in the trough. There's money in building new houses.'

'I'm not sure ...'

'You mean you're frightened.' She held his look, then smiled at him.

He blushed. 'Got a pen?'

She handed one over.

He got out his wallet and wrote on the back of a receipt. 'I'll see what I can do. Here's my mobile number.

Ring me if you need help.' He handed over the piece of paper. Best change the subject. 'So you can't help me with who might have murdered John?'

'I haven't had a normal face-to-face conversation with him in years, just harassment from a distance. It's easy if you can't look a person in the eye, isn't it? If we'd met face-to-face I'd have likely murdered him myself.' She put her glass down and smiled at him. 'How about you? Are you in a relationship?'

He held her gaze. 'Not just at the moment. And you?'

'Same. It's difficult to find anyone reasonable. I tried *The Guardian* lonely hearts page, but they all described themselves as tall, dark and handsome and fun people but turned out to be short, bald, ugly psychopaths.' She laughed. 'And miserable with it.'

She stood, pulled on a white raincoat and slipped on a pair of black, high-heeled shoes. In them she seemed a foot taller. 'I'm afraid I've got to love you and leave you,' she said. 'Got to do some shopping before the meeting.' She turned and gave him another smile. 'I always liked you, Martin. Always laughing and joking. Maybe we could go on a date like we were teenagers again, or maybe you could come round for a meal, bring a bottle of Rioja. That would be a lark, wouldn't it?'

He tried to hold his cool but failed and threw a coughing fit. 'Have you ever read David Copperfield?' he eventually managed to splutter.

'What? I've seen it on the telly ...'

'Barkis is willing.'

CHAPTER TWELVE

'Settled in okay? James not being too irritating?'

Jane took a sip of her coffee and looked around. The snack bar was close to the office and did a brisk trade in sandwiches and Americanos. There were no free tables, so they had to sit on stools at a narrow bar by the entrance. Busy but not so busy as to start her off. She screwed up her face in answer to Cath's question. 'No more passes. Yet.'

Cath laughed. 'He even tried it on with me,' she said. 'Luckily he's not my line manager. Yet. Look, Jane, James had a chat with me this morning. Seems like you've been having some disagreements. What's going on?'

Jane stared at her. 'You know what he's like: gives out this air of being the modern boss, but underneath he's a power freak. I'm afraid I was spoilt in my previous job ...'

'That was in Birmingham, wasn't it? Weren't you a planner? You were brought in to bring some expertise to James's team when he took over responsibility for planning.'

'That's right. I was a member of a management team that worked well together. We could discuss things and disagree but still be friends afterwards. If someone doesn't agree with what you're saying it's not always a power play on their part. You might simply be wrong.'

'Exactly. Why did you leave if it was so good?'

Jane sighed. Cath might be a friend, but she was still Head of HR. What had Jane put on her application form? Some shit about 'new challenges'.

'It was my home life,' Jane said. 'Not the job. I needed a change.'

Cath's eyebrows rose.

'I'm not saying any more,' Jane said.

'Okay.' Cath thought for a while. 'What do you think of these latest council plans? They're talking about selling off the Hatton Garden office for conversion to flats.'

'And the Municipal Annexe for conversion to a hotel.'

'Isn't that building listed?' Cath asked.

'Yeah, but the interested developers say they can keep the character.'

'And I thought the office was about to fall down.'

'They reckon it can be repaired and sold on as a viable proposition, but what'll happen to all the people who work there?'

'What do you think? Soon you'll be sitting by yourself watching the tumbleweed roll down the aisles. Nearly everyone who works there is dead wood—apart from you, of course—sick, lame and lazy. Sent by other departments throughout the city to while away the time to the next cull. Don't quote me on that, but it's common knowledge.'

'Well, it can't come too soon for some of them. They need to be put out of their misery. Thanks for landing me with Ann Smith, by the way. I asked for a support team, not a sabotage team.'

'Having problems?'

'Problems? She won't do anything. She's very polite about it. All I get is, "I'd prefer not to". In the army she'd have been taken out and shot.'

'I'm sorry, I thought she might've been some help. She spent thirty years photocopying in the legal department; now the solicitors type it themselves or more usually just change a standard document, then they print it out. There are things you can try ...'

'What? Like reasoning with her? Trying to instil some team spirit? I've tried it all. She doesn't fit into the usual categories of difficult staff. And it's especially hard if you've inherited them. You can be as compassionate and understanding as you like, but if they won't obey orders there's nothing you can do. They know it's a temporary arrangement and that you're not a proper line manager and can't discipline them. And it's disruptive for the other team members to see someone getting away with murder. It rankles.'

Cath nodded. 'So where do you disagree with James?' she asked after a while.

'Oh, it's this strategic thing: encouraging private housing development; building on the green belt and the green wedges. And then there's the Irish Streets thing.'

'The Irish Streets? But isn't that what you want? Rather than building in the green belt, build on brownfield land?'

'The Streets aren't brownfield land. Though Whitaker and his supporters would like it to be. It's a community, and the houses aren't ready for demolition. Most of them could be refurbished. It's about bringing yuppies with jobs who pay their council tax into the city.'

'It's all over the papers. Can't you compromise?'

Jane shrugged. 'I would. I've looked at the demand for housing; it's not so great that you couldn't go at a gentler pace. But, no; James wants to go hell for leather.'

'Hell for leather? Why would that be?'

'What do you mean, why would that be? He thinks it'll get him re-elected. Though I'm not so sure. People care more about bin collections and dogs crapping on the pavements than housing policy …' Jane considered Cath. Could she trust her?

'This increase in his powers has gone to his head,' Jane continued, her voice low now. 'I don't know what possessed this government to give him control of the whole of transport, economic development and business in Merseyside over the heads of the local politicians, and they took the planning powers from them and gave them to him. It's devolution made to look silly.'

'Doesn't the Secretary of State have to rubber stamp any decisions?'

'Yes, it's got to look reasonable and above board, but still … basically, Whitaker's promised to get all these houses built, and the only way he could do that is by building in the green belt. He hasn't got long now before the election, and all the other candidates have promised to revoke his powers if they take control.' Jane paused.

'The thing is,' she continued, 'his ambitions go be-yond mayor of Merseyside. He's been secretly talking to

UKIP about standing as an MP. He would lead a charge at the government on the rate of housebuilding. He performs so well on the telly. He's got the establishment worried.' She paused again. 'So you could say that we disagree on certain matters.' Jane looked around the snack bar and recognised a face from work. It was too dangerous to talk openly here. Cath followed her look.

'Look,' Cath said. 'We can't talk here. Do you fancy a drink after work?'

*

The office had been created by knocking three shops into one. A big sign went right across all three: *MERSEY ESTATES*. White on red. Bang in the middle of Childwall. Inside, real oak flooring, bright lighting, but not too bright, and red leather sofas. Property details covered every inch of wall space. The manager's office was all glass, like a goldfish bowl, so he could keep an eye on the comings and goings. The three salespersons sat behind desks.

'Raymond popped out?' Jimmy said.

Janice, the nearest salesperson, looked up. 'Yes,' she said. 'Checking properties.'

Jimmy didn't believe her. He picked up an *Echo* from a table and scanned through. Ah, there it was. Car auction at a garage on Smithdown Road. The question was, should he track down and confront his Childwall branch manager? Sack him on the spot? That was what he deserved. Cheeky, cocky little arsehole with his Count Dracula hairstyle and his fancy duds. It would be too much trouble at the moment. Save it for later.

His mobile went.

'A'right there, Hughesy!'

Chuckie. What a place to call. Jimmy walked outside, looking around. Several buses were going by. That would drown out any surveillance. He walked along the pavement. 'Chuckie?' he said as calmly as he could into the mobile.

'How's it going, lar? Just checking up. Appeal's going well. Might be out in a few months. How's the nest egg going?'

'Fine, fine. Look ...' An empty space grew in Jimmy's guts.

'Don't want to know the details, kid. Can't stay long on here. Keep up the good work. England expects and all that! Chin, chin!'

*

Malone leaned forward, his spiky hairstyle bobbing up and down. Was it a rug? He wore chinos, a checked shirt and fancy, pointy brown shoes. Jimmy was aware of the contrast between Malone's stylish clothes and his own green, waxed Barbour jacket and boring suit—the sort of stuff you picked up in Asda if you wanted to look like an accountant.

'This knobhead courier, Hardin,' Malone said, 'claimed that he was robbed of the gear and the cash. It was supposed to be a routine swop. I didn't believe him, obviously, but before I could look into it, he dies of a heart attack on the escalator in the Royal. In front of maybe fifty people.'

The sun was out, and quite a few families walked by the Sefton Park lake, some eating ice creams. A big commotion came from the entrance—squawking and quacking. Someone was feeding bread to the ducks. On the shallow lake several nests floated, little built-up islands of vegetation with coots and ducks bobbing backwards and forwards. No one within earshot.

'Very convenient,' Jimmy said. 'The thing is, Michael, I asked you to run down that side of the business.'

'I am running it down. This was the last run. We were contractually committed to the fellers over there.'

'Well, they're not going to be happy with this, are they?'

'Too right. We're looking everywhere. Searched his flat. Found nothing.'

'Well, search it again. Have you checked his relatives, friends, people who might've been in on it?'

'He was a bit of a loner. Alky and a druggy. There was someone with him in the hospital cafe before it happened. Ran to him when he was slumped on the escalator. The cops have got him on CCTV and they've interviewed him. Once we get his name and where he lives we'll pay him a visit and find out what he knows.'

'The thing is, Michael,' Jimmy said, 'those fellers on the other side of the pond. They don't like this. It's not so much the money as the loss of face. They don't mess about, them folk. So how did they get my phone number at home? They rang me in the middle of a family meal and told me that if I didn't get the money and the stuff back in a week I was a dead man. The cheeky gits; they were laughing at me, Michael ...'

'I don't ...'

'I'll be a laughing stock in Liverpool if anyone hears about this. And to cap it all, the plods and the feds are really cracking down on drugs and the violent stuff at the moment.'

'I know that. I'll sort this; don't worry.'

Neither man said anything for a while. They watched a pair of coots fight and splash next to a nest.

'And what about this business on the front page of the *Echo* the other night?'

'What business? The Queen Mary visit?'

'No, the lad crucified in the park.'

'Nothing to do with me, that.'

Silence for a full minute, then Malone giggled. 'The grass had it coming, didn't he?'

Silence for another minute.

'The thing is, Michael,' Jimmy said at last, 'it's a tricky time at the moment. We've got some big deals going through. Legitimate deals. The last thing we need is any embarrassment. We're still trying to live down the last mess. The South Americans get really pissed off when someone grasses. It wasn't even my uncle, but he got the blame. Stitched his face onto a football and threw it on to Chuckie during a five-a-side game in the exercise yard of the strictest prison in Europe.'

'I know. Bad do, that. The plods and the feds were all over us like a rash. Or a plague, more like. Took a long time for things to settle down.'

'So the word from Chuckie is to get out of the bad stuff and build up some nice legitimate businesses. When you've sorted this out, we'll fix you up with a nice comfortable job. How would you like to look after the property portfolio?'

'Collecting rents? That's not me, Jimmy.'

'Well, what about the massage parlours?'

'I'm not a ponce.'

Jimmy examined Micky. He looked like a ponce. But he liked the buzz too much—taking risks, running round town in a fast car with a pistol in the dashboard and an Uzi in the boot. Maybe the answer was to cut him adrift, let him go his own way with the drugs and the violence. But there was no guarantee he wouldn't cause them trouble in some way. He was that sort of character. Trouble.

'Okay, we'll think of something,' Jimmy said. 'But cut down on the violence and keep us off the front page of the *Echo*. Do your best to sort things out. Give your Irish friends what they want, then cut it off completely. And try not to use too much violence. Am I making myself clear? Sort things out.'

'And if I don't? What are you going to do about it?'

Jimmy turned and glared at Micky, trying to look tough. He wasn't sure about what he saw in Micky's bright blue eyes. Amusement? Contempt, even. Jimmy turned away.

There was a long pause. Two ducks started a fight on the lake right in front of them, splashing and quacking.

*

James Whitaker was late. He parked the limo on Mossley Hill Drive and sat for a few minutes to check that he wasn't being followed or, just as bad, recognised as the mayor by some balloonhead.

No one about. He got out of the car, carrying the paper and the pack of sandwiches. Lunch in the park. What could be more normal? It took him about five minutes to walk over to the mound overlooking the lake where the seat was. Clear view all round. Far enough from any trees or bushes.

Carter was there, eating sandwiches and reading a paper. Seedy-looking. As ever. With his money you'd have thought he could afford a new suit and look the part of a big-time lawyer.

'Afternoon,' Whitaker said. 'Mind if I join you? How are tricks?'

Carter looked up from the paper and stared ahead, his face expressionless. *Daily Telegraph.* Whitaker could tell by the print even though it was folded.

'So, so. Business could be better.'

Whitaker laughed. 'I know. I read about it in the papers. So what's so urgent? These face-to-face meetings are very risky.'

'Ha, ha. Not as risky as talking over the phone. I could do with some action on the Mersey Estates land.'

'You mean you need the money. Well, that'll take a bit of time. Steady as she goes.'

Carter turned. His face had a hint of redness. 'Steady

as she goes? When the ship's going down? Don't forget that I've got enough on you, Mr James Whitaker, to take you down with me!'

'What exactly do you mean by that, Benny? I'm surprised at you. I thought we were colleagues. And friends.'

'I'm just saying that if the going gets rough, then I've got all the evidence safely locked away. Stuff from the old days. I took the precaution of taking copies. It's like an insurance policy.' He stared at something in the distance. 'Oh, fuck. We'll have to go.' He stood. 'We'll need another venue.'

*

Someone had been using the cul-de-sac as a rubbish tip: cone-shaped piles of old tarmac, bricks and rubble obviously dumped off the back of a tipper lorry; mountains of black plastic bin bags, some split open to reveal rusty cans; pages of newspaper; empty milk cartons, and from it all sprouted a surprising variety of weeds and tiny trees.

Jimmy tried to scrabble his way through, but his feet slipped on the plastic and soil mixed with rotting paper, and he nearly fell into the mess. A strong stench of decay rose from the split bags when he disturbed them. He tried around one side and had to pull a couple of bin bags away but managed to reach the wooden doors to the lockup. The faded green paint had peeled off them, leaving grey wood, and the bottoms were rotting away.

A big rusty padlock secured the door. He'd come prepared with a pair of bolt clippers and a small jemmy. A couple of twists of the jemmy and the hasp wrenched off. He pulled the door until he could just squeeze in. A white Escort van covered in a layer of dust with no number plates was rusting away and taking up most of the garage. The place smelt of engine oil and decay.

At the back of the garage, cobwebs almost completely covered a window, but it let in enough light to see a rack of shelves with rusting tins and a greasy canvas bag about five feet long on the bottom shelf. He unzipped it, revealing several longish objects wrapped in plastic. He peered at one. From the shape and weight it looked like a Kalashnikov. Several bags of what looked like ammunition clips lay beside it.

This was no use; too big and clumsy. He rooted through the bag, and in a corner he found a small parcel—tiny compared to the others. He ripped open the plastic. A small automatic sat inside, heavier than it looked and oily to the touch. Full magazine.

This was more like it. Nearly as small as a mobile phone, it could almost pass for a kiddy's toy, but on closer inspection it was obviously real. Perfect for personal protection. But easily mislaid. He'd have to find a safe place for it.

He slipped the gun into his pocket and walked back outside. The garages backed onto the Pools building site. He managed to scramble along one side on a track which led to a wire fence that had been cut and peeled back. This must be where the scallies gained access to the site. Anything that could be sold for scrap had been stripped and robbed: electric cable, heating pipes, radiators. There was supposed to be on-site security, but he saw no signs of life as he walked across what had been a car park to the shell of the building. Clumps of brambles and little trees coming up to his waist, bricks, lengths of rusty pipe and large pools of water almost obscured the tarmac.

Every window in the building had been smashed, and graffiti covered the exterior walls. Anything metal was rusting away. Maybe a body could be hidden here? He stopped at a drainage chamber that had lost its lid. He couldn't see the bottom. He dropped a pebble in, and it was a few seconds before he heard a splash. The problem would be getting a vehicle in. The gates were padlocked. Maybe not.

CHAPTER THIRTEEN

'I'm sorry, Mr Bennett, but Mrs Bennett doesn't want to see you.'

The receptionist put the phone down and regarded Martin. She seemed very young for the job—small, thin and with a blonde ponytail, more like a schoolgirl.

He couldn't think of a thing to say. In the end, he muttered something and beat a retreat, sure that his cheeks were red.

He walked out of the hospital and back along the road. An eight-foot-high sandstone boundary wall enclosed the grounds with a line of mature trees immediately inside. He tried to remember where her room was, made his best guess and clambered up onto the wall. Beyond the line of trees was shrubbery, well-kept lawns and flower beds with a two-storey buff brick building beyond. To one side sat a small lake with some reeds on the edge and a couple of ducks dabbling in the water—everything quiet and peaceful. No one around.

He lowered himself down the other side, dropped to the ground and squatted for a moment in the shade of a large tree. Twigs and leaves sprinkled the bare, sandy earth. He strolled along the side of the building, trying to appear as nonchalant as possible.

Julie lay in a recliner on the patio outside her room. She looked to be asleep.

Martin was taken aback by how bad his ex-wife looked. Julie was ill, true, but it was supposed to be mental, not physical. Her long hair, which had once been raven black with a glossy sheen, was now grey and dead-looking. Her face looked thinner; her whole body looked thinner. And she had greenish-grey patches under her eyes.

But it wasn't his fault, was it? Debbie, his daughter, was fair to him, but still tended to take her mother's side. Deep down he knew he'd done nothing wrong, that he'd remained faithful to that ideal conception of himself that every man sets up for himself, secretly. But what Julie had said had planted a heavy dart in his heart: "You've got nothing I want. You can leave if you want to."

She opened her eyes and yawned. He sat on a chair a few feet away. She moved up on the recliner so she could look at him.

'Oh, it's you,' she said, her voice so low he could hardly hear her.

They sat in silence for a while. A duck quacked a couple of times. Silence again. A bird sang in the near distance, a lovely loud and clear warbling.

'Is that a skylark?' he said.

'Yes; there's an open field at the back. Nice, isn't it? It used to be the playing field when this place was a school. They're going to develop it soon. It's a shame. The singing cheers you up.'

Martin thought for a while. 'Remember when we used to walk through the woods at Formby to the sea?' he said. 'You used to get skylarks singing over the heathland there, didn't you?'

She leaned back and closed her eyes.

'Debbie used to collect cones,' he said, 'and we picked blackberries. The apple and blackberry pie you made was nicer than the wine I made.' He paused. 'People don't make wine and pies from blackberries and apples these days. You can buy wine and fruit pies so cheap in the supermarket that there's no point. And there was always the risk that the wine would go off and you would have to pour it down the sink.'

'It was so cool in those pine woods,' she said. 'I can smell it now. What was that smell? Like cough sweets.'

'Resin. It was the resin from the pine trees.'

'And Debbie got caught by that wave.'

'Knocked her off her feet. She went right in. Soaked to the skin. When you look at her now it's difficult to imagine that I used to carry her around in a baby harness. Carried her up Scafell inside my shirt. It was raining, blowing a gale, but she was as snug as a bug in a rug. Then there was that time at Church Meadow when she tried to get the feather in the lake and fell in. I jumped in in my clothes, but it was only about a foot deep.'

'So what brings you here?' she said. 'It's not bad news, is it?'

'Only for John Hardin.'

'What's happened?'

'He's back in Liverpool. He's been murdered.'

She opened her eyes. 'Murdered?'

'Yeah. I'm trying to find out who did it.'

'I thought you hated him.'

'I do. But that's the point.'

She sat up straight. 'So why are you here?' Her voice rose with every word. 'Do you think I had something to do with it? From a hospital bed?'

'No, I thought he might have contacted you.'

'You what!' she shouted. 'Contacted me! You've got a cheek coming here!' She turned and pressed a bell on the wall.

A male nurse in green overalls burst through the door. He was tall, maybe six feet four, and heavy with it, more like a bouncer than a nurse. His big face screwed up with concern.

'Julie?' he said. 'What's the problem?'

'Thank God you came, Ron. He's my ex-husband and he's threatening me again.'

Martin tried to protest, but the nurse took Martin's arm in a powerful grip, then, without any fuss, guided him towards the way out.

'Julie's told me about you,' the man said in his ear. Close enough for Martin to get a thick waft of what he'd had for lunch—something garlicky and meaty. 'You're the one who put her in here. Who caused her to do what she did. You're responsible for it all.'

Martin twisted until he could look at the man, their faces inches apart. 'You've only heard her side of it,' Martin said. 'You must know about her condition. She makes things up. There're always two sides to anything like this. I admit that I behaved badly, but she wasn't blameless ...'

The man considered him for a moment. Martin saw

the doubt in his eyes. The moment passed, and the man assumed the stern expression again.

'I'm going to say this once and once only,' he said, his voice low. A drop of spittle splashed into Martin's face. 'If I set eyes on you again, I'll call the police.'

CHAPTER FOURTEEN

Shouts echoed around the hall from a demonstration outside the community centre. Jane Trevelyan was by now familiar with the signs of a panic attack—fast breathing, sweating, acute discomfort—but she also knew there was little she could do about it. She skipped away from the group of officials and into the toilet where she quickly swallowed a couple of tablets with a gulp of water from a tap.

This had all started with finding the lump on Bruce that morning. Golden retrievers were susceptible to mast cell tumours. Several had been removed in the past, and they had all turned out to be benign, but there was always the chance that one would turn out to be aggressive. She'd made an appointment with the vet for that afternoon, and she would just have to go—no point in asking Whitaker for permission. She walked back into the hall.

He was about to start. Her boss cut an impressive figure at the podium: tall, swept back dark hair with grey streaks; well-fitting dark blue suit, pale blue shirt, understated dark red tie; perfect image. Toadies, sycophants and journalists filled the seats directly in front of him.

'Good evening, ladies and gentleman. I am James Whitaker, mayor of Liverpool, and I'm here today to announce a new programme to regenerate this city, the first since I was granted planning powers by the government. The residents of the Irish Streets have waited long enough for the investment this area desperately needs. They have shown fantastic community spirit in fighting for a future in which there will be no more derelict sites and boarded-up properties. We have worked closely with the developers, the council and the community to come up with a project that we fully believe meets the needs and aspirations of the people.'

The lights went out and everyone's attention was drawn to the projected image on the screen above Whitaker—a brightly coloured master plan of the area.

'The survey shows that there is little interest in old terraced houses from first-time buyers and renters,' came Whitaker's voice-over. 'They are not energy-efficient and, of course, you don't have car parking and gardens for children to play safely. Refurb some of the old terraces, certainly. But what we need is a mix of housing and a more balanced community.' He paused. 'We will build a hundred and fifty new homes, demolish three hundred and refurbish fifty—all at a cost of fifteen million pounds—and create new green open spaces.'

He paused to let this sink in. The lights came on, and he looked around the audience. He certainly looked the part in his beautifully tailored suit, beautifully barbered hair and beautifully tanned skin. Many women found him irresistibly attractive, but he just wasn't Jane's type. Something she'd tried to get over to him several times but failed.

'No family these days wants to live in a terraced property,' he said. 'Families want gardens and driveways. Okay, some will want terraced property, and we will save and refurbish a number of the best properties, but to create a thriving city we need a good mix of housing, and to achieve that we need family homes. Option One.' The plan on the screen showed the Irish Streets area with various blocks of colour superimposed. 'This was to be total demolition and rebuild. Option two.' The slide changed. 'Involves the retention of a third of the houses—restored by a housing association—and the rest redeveloped, with an area retained for public open space.'

'Who will build these new houses?' a youngish man who was standing in the aisle near the front shouted.

'There'll be time for questions at the end, Angus,' Whitaker said with a smile.

'Come on, who will build them?' the man shouted, moving forward. 'It wouldn't be one of your crony companies, would it?'

'Okay, Angus, we're familiar with your objections to everything we're trying to do, which you express so eloquently in your column. I don't think many of the people who will benefit from this project read *The Guardian*—'

'Never mind that; just answer the question. Who will make the big money out of this?'

A young man ran forward. 'It's social cleansing! Like the Nazis. Get rid of the working class, bring in the toffs!'

The hall erupted with shouts and banging of chairs.

Whitaker nodded towards the rear of the hall. A couple of stewards quickly advanced on the protestor, hooked an arm under each of his and carried him from the room, shouting loudly as he went.

'This is typical strong-arm tactics!' said a confident female voice. 'Just like the militant days!' The speaker was a striking-looking lady with short, well-cut blonde hair. She wore a white mac over a black top, black slacks and black high-heeled shoes. She'd obviously worked hard on the model image. Jane could never be bothered. This woman looked tall in heels but would be the same height as Jane in the comfortable flats Jane wore now.

A pair of men sitting next to where the lady stood in the aisle turned to each other. One made a surreptitious figure-of-eight gesture like in a *Carry On* film.

'Are you going to deny that you have links to the local construction industry?' the lady shouted.

'What are you inferring, madam? Of course we have links with the local construction industry. That's how things get built!'

'I'm inferring that you are corrupt and that this whole project is corrupt.'

'Thank you, madam,' Whitaker said. 'If you would kindly leave your name and contact details with one of the officers at the back of the hall, then my solicitors can be in touch with you to discuss the procedure whereby we can take you to court for slander.' He nodded to the stewards, who advanced on the lady.

'Don't you touch me, you shaved ape!' she shouted as the first one tried to take her arm. 'You look like a bouncer. Is there no work on the doors, then? Touch me and I'll dump you on your arse like a sack of spuds!'

The hall erupted with laughter, cheering, clapping and stamping of feet.

'Good for you, gerl!'

Eventually she sat down with her chin up and her arms folded. The stewards retreated.

'Now,' Whitaker said, 'as I was saying before I was so rudely interrupted, local people are at the heart of everything we're doing. We know from our extensive consultation that the vast majority are in favour of our plans. They're fed up with the delays and just want us to get on with delivering the new homes they want. There will always be cynics and jeremiahs no matter what you do, so let's just get on with it.'

Jane couldn't stand the crowded room any longer and went out the back way to have a sly fag. She tried to ignore the chanting from the front of the centre. After a few puffs she managed to calm herself down enough to go back in.

A lady opposition councillor—young, dark, attractive and well-dressed—was giving it loads as she usually did. You could set your watch by her.

'And, Mr Mayor, I conclude by saying that I and the Lib Dems will do whatever we can to support the local community in their stand against you!'

Loud cheering and applause.

'Thanks for that, Harriet!' Whitaker shouted over the applause, beaming and clapping himself. 'No change and well turned out as usual!'

'Mr Mayor!'

A thickset man in a dark blue suit and a shiny bald

head stood in the aisle.

'Ah, Tommy,' Whitaker said, as if greeting a close friend. 'I wondered when you were going to stick your oar in.'

'Mr Mayor! If no one knows who I am …' His eyes roved over the audience. 'I am Councillor Tommy Kelly. Leader of the Labour Group on the council.'

'And mayoral candidate,' Whitaker said, laughing. 'Don't forget that.'

'That's right, mayoral candidate. I think the people have had enough of a know-nothing as mayor. The novelty's worn off if you hadn't noticed.' He walked a couple of paces forward. 'Can I make a solemn pledge to the people who live in the Irish Streets?' He paused. Whitaker regarded him with mock curiosity. 'When I become mayor, my first act will be to revoke the proposals for this area. We will not demolish one dwelling. Not one. We will renovate the lot. Lock, stock and barrel!'

'And what about UKIP!' shouted someone from the back of the hall.

Whitaker stared into the darkness. Jane had to stop herself from laughing out loud. The UK Independence Party had targeted Liverpool but their message of anti-immigration and of leaving the European Union had not gone down as well as they had hoped.

'You've been talking to UKIP, haven't you!' yelled the heckler. 'Dickhead!'

Whitaker tried to respond, but the cheering, shouting and stamping of feet was too loud. Jane had to get out.

CHAPTER FIFTEEN

'It must be hard not being allowed to drive,' Debbie said. Her long blonde hair glowed in the light from the candles on the table of the Warrington wine bar. Martin's heart skipped a beat. She was so beautiful. And intelligent. And a good person. He always respected her opinions and trusted her judgement. It was difficult to believe she was the product of his loins, carrying his seed into the future.

'It's okay,' he said. 'It's not too bad by train. Quick bus ride to Hunts Cross and Bob's your uncle. It's a chance to bring my knowledge of public transport in Merseyside up to date.'

He looked around. The place was half full. Subdued lights. Low buzz of conversation. Lots of mirrors. Music playing but not too loud. Was that Dylan? *House of the Rising Sun* from his first album. Very tasteful. The staff as jovial as could be expected on the minimum wage. He'd heard a central European inflection in the girl's voice when she'd welcomed them. Polish? The pair had attracted one or two glances when they'd arrived. Moll with her sugar daddy twice her age? Nah. Middle-aged dad with daughter.

'How long will it last for?'

'A month or two. I go in for a check-up in a couple of weeks.'

'And are you feeling okay in yourself?'

'Never felt better. Just got to keep taking the tablets. Eat better. Get more exercise.'

'Will you stick to it, though? I know what you're like!'

'Of course I will. It's taught me a lesson, all this. I've even gone vegetarian like you. Started eating salads. Given up the booze and the fags.'

'I was wondering why you ordered the veggie option.'

The food arrived. True to his promise, he had lasagne with salad. No chips. Debbie had the same.

'I'm halfway through *A Brief History of Time*,' he said. His fork hovered over a lettuce leaf. 'I can understand the special theory and even the general theory, but I can't get my head around quantum theory.'

She laughed. 'Come on, Dad, I bought that book for your birthday three months ago. You asked for it.'

'I'm trying. I want to understand it. It's easy for you. Physics lecturer with a PhD. But I'm a past-it punter. Failed my physics O level. I can handle the idea of two balls of different weights falling at the same speed. I can just about handle time dilation. But the idea that you can't be certain of the position or velocity of anything is just too much.'

'Best not to worry about it. It's just theoretical stuff that works at the sub-atomic level. It doesn't apply in everyday life. See that tomato?' She pointed. 'I aim my fork at it just so and it's where I expect it to be. You don't need quantum theory.' She speared the tomato and popped it into her mouth. 'Down the hatch. Same as time dilation. It only works when you are going very fast. Even if you take a trip to the moon at thirty thousand miles an hour it's not fast enough for the effect to kick in.'

'I know. But it's just the thought that everything is uncertain that bugs me. That nothing is what it seems, everything is accicental. That there's no underlying order.' He paused. 'John Hardin, a fellow I used to climb with, died recently. Most likely murdered. No apparent motive. You probably don't remember him.' He studied her face.

'Yes, I do. He was one of your climbing mates. You say he was murdered?'

'Yeah. I met him at the hospital when they diagnosed the stroke. I'd not seen him for years. We talked over a coffee.' He paused and laughed. 'I know this sounds far-fetched, but he had what looked like a heart attack on the escalator. But I saw someone push something into him, a needle or something.'

'Didn't you go to the police?'

'Yeah. But he was cremated in a rush. Something's going on, and I'm trying to find out what it is.'

She laughed. 'Come on, Dad. Like a private investigator or something? You're supposed to be recovering from a stroke. You can't go round pretending to be Gumshoe or Columbo.'

He stared at her. 'I found your mother's telephone number on his iPad and some pictures of you.'

It was her turn to stare at him. 'Pictures of me? But I don't even know him.'

145

'I asked your mother. We had a nice chat about old times. Like when you fell in the lake when we were camping, stretching to get the feather. And how I used to carry you up mountains inside my shirt when you were a baby. And how it didn't seem like no time at all before I was having to pick you up from night clubs in town at two in the morning.' He stopped talking at the sight of anger in her face.

'Oh, Dad!' she cried. 'You haven't been upsetting Mum again. God knows what she might do. You promised.' She burst into tears. People at other tables turned their way. After a while, she got a tissue from her bag and wiped her eyes, then she pulled out a mobile and rang a number. 'Gerry, can you pick me up now?'

'Come on, Debbie,' Martin said. 'We've only just started the meal.'

She turned away. They both picked at their food, without eating.

A few minutes later, she looked up towards the entrance, then stood and put her coat on. Martin turned. Her partner stood by the door with a questioning look on his face. He must have been waiting not far away.

*

Martin just missed the train back and had a long wait on the station with only the rainy night for company—plenty of time to ponder on the depressing turn in his investigation. When he got home, he took off his coat and trudged upstairs to collapse in the chair in front of the wall. It glistened with moisture. The patch of black fungus by the chimney breast was getting bigger. It happened every time it rained.

After a few minutes, he got up and taped up the sheet of wallpaper. Three leads, three dead ends—two of them emotional disasters. After the do with Debbie, he'd run into a brick wall. There was no point ringing the hospital—they wouldn't put him through to Julie. And after what that male nurse had said, they wouldn't let him in the door.

He felt a strong urge to give up, just go to sleep for as long as it took. He considered the list. One name might merit further investigation.

A loud wailing sound came from the other side of the wall.

'I-ee-I-ee-I will always love you!'

'Right, that's it!' he yelled. He ran over to the box of CDs and rifled through, found the one he wanted and put it on.

Jackhammer guitars and power drumming exploded from the player—from the Eighties and not one of Lester's CDs, but fuck it. He turned it to maximum volume and placed it on the floor next to the wall.

'If you like to gamble, I tell you I'm your man ...'

The voice was hoarse and world-weary. Yep, good old Lemmy would sort them out.

CHAPTER SIXTEEN

'So how's it going?' Cath asked.

She looked different out of her work clothes, more sophisticated, less the sensible human relations person. Cath was roughly ten years younger than Jane, most likely in her late thirties but not so much younger that she made Jane feel like an old hag.

The atmosphere in the pub was relaxing: low modern jazz music and a background of conversation, but not too busy. Towards the end of the after-work rush hour. The office workers were going home, and the evening clientele hadn't started to arrive yet. And the rain would put a lot of people off. Perfect for a head-to-head. Jane wouldn't have come otherwise.

Cath took a sip of her wine. They were sharing a bottle of red. 'Are you settled in? Where is it you're living? Woolton?'

'The house is a bit of a boring semi. A bit big for a single person. But it'll do for now. Quite handy for the bus and the train. So I don't have to use the car that much. It's got a nice back garden so Bruce is happy enough. And the park's close by. The problem is finding time to give him a good run. Golden retrievers need their exercise. Too often it's gone dark by the time I get home. I have to walk him by the light of a torch.'

Cath nodded.

'And you? How's the family?' Jane asked.

'Oh, you know. Two kids at junior school. Not enough hours in the day,' Cath said. 'And they're starting to do things at night. Swimming, football, things they need chauffeuring to and from.' She took a sip of wine and looked at Jane. 'I checked your application form. You answered "none" to the medical conditions question.'

Jane said nothing. Her heart raced, and a cold sweat spread throughout her body.

'I checked it out,' Cath continued. 'You signed a waiver allowing us to check with your GP. It used to take a fortnight—now we do it digitally and it takes ten minutes. You've been having treatment for panic attacks and depression. You've been prescribed medication and therapy.' She smiled. 'We've had our fingers burned so many times in this line of work that we've put systems in place to counter abuse.' She smiled again. 'Tell me what happened, Jane.'

Jane closed her eyes and tried to contain the panic attack. This was a nightmare. But Cath seemed so sympathetic, maybe she'd see it from Jane's point of view.

'I've always liked going for long walks in the country by myself,' Jane said. 'I was bullied at school. I was a little swot. Top of the class. The other girls didn't like it. I needed to escape. Hence the long walks in the country. Anyway, when I was fifteen I went on a long walk by a river. Through woods, meadows, wildflowers. It was beautiful.'

'It sounds it,' Cath said.

'Yes. Then it started to rain. I was only wearing a summer dress and sandals. It got worse and worse until I was soaked to the skin. The stepping stones I'd used to cross the river an hour earlier were covered by the water. I was trudging down the road when this Land Rover came by with an old farmer inside. Tweeds, cap, pipe. Really friendly. Gave me a lift. He was chatting all the way. Took me to a farmhouse. Gave me a towel and told me to dry off in front of the open fire. Then he sat next to me. Put his hand on my leg and tried to kiss me. I ran for it. Eventually found a bus stop.' She took a deep breath.

Cath looked outraged.

'Ever since then I've distrusted men,' Jane continued. 'Even when I went to university. I had the odd boyfriend, but nothing much. Then when I started working, I was successful in my job. Eventually I became the head of a Planning department. I met a nice man there, but it didn't work out. So there I was. Divorced, no kids. Met Steven on an internet dating site. At first, he seemed to be the perfect partner. Charming, considerate. Told me he worked as a financial adviser and ran his own company, but it turned out that he'd been made redundant from a job in a car showroom. God knows what he's doing now. Probably got a job as a bouncer.' She laughed.

'When I first met him,' she continued, 'he had a good physique—one of the things I liked about him. But he started going down the gym all the time and shifting weights. Obsessive. Became a muscleman. Like those idiots you see on TV. He'd had a string of violent relationships. Two divorces. Four kids. He was supposed to be supporting them, but he was on the run from the authorities. He had no qualifications and huge debts from betting. He was very clever, but the mask always slips. I confronted him with his lies and everything went downhill from that point. He attacked me and I got a court order to throw him out. He harassed me. Emails, phone calls.'

'It sounds awful.'

'It was a nightmare. I started to notice that he'd been in the house. Things moved. Underwear stolen. I had to get the locks changed. Then he parked his car outside my workplace with blow-up photographs in the windows with the caption: *Jane Trevelyan—whore.*

'He'd photoshopped my face onto pornstars doing disgusting things. It wasn't even a professional job. You could see the joins. But everyone at work thought it was hilarious.'

'Didn't you tell the police?'

'Of course. He was warned, but he came back and attacked me. Broke in and raped me. He got six years, but he was out in less than two. That's when the panic attacks started. I was totally paranoid. I had to move somewhere far away even if it meant a demotion and less money. I can't appear in the press or on TV. He'd track me down. This seemed like the perfect backroom job.'

'It's hardly that,' Cath said. 'The mayor's in the public eye.'

'I know. But I thought I'd be doing research in a back room. It's not easy.'

Cath nodded.

'What are you going to do?' Jane asked.

'Do? Nothing. I just need some help.'

'Help? What sort of help?'

'You have access to James's computer system. I need to know who he's been in contact with regarding the green belt and Irish Streets projects. This has been cleared at the highest level. Help us out on this and we'll overlook the application form.'

Jane thought for a few moments. 'So in return for not giving me the sack,' she said. 'You want me to hack into my manager's computer system?'

'That's about the size of it.'

CHAPTER SEVENTEEN

He'd taken a risk driving. He hadn't been signed off by a doctor. But this lead seemed the only viable one left. What would be the penalty if he were caught? A heavy fine and a long ban, probably.

He drove over the brow of a hill just before Ceregydrudion and came upon a grand panorama of the mountains of Snowdonia. Snowdon itself, the Glyders, Tryfan and the Carneds, the blue remembered hills of Martin's first visits to the area many years before. A few years ago some idiot of a famous climber had said in an interview, 'Who cares about the view?'

'Well, I care about the view, you uneducated philistine!' Martin had shouted out loud on reading it.

The next straight section was the 'hundred miles an hour bit' when Lester used to hoot loudly and accelerate the Vincent motorbike hard while Martin clutched the sides of the seat and closed his eyes. Once he'd opened them and glanced over Lester's shoulder. The bike really was doing a hundred miles an hour. The Toyota Martin was driving now couldn't match that. Nowhere near.

Next came the A5 and a long straight road with the mountains getting steadily closer. Finally, the road began to wind through the forests before the village of Betwys y Coed. Then the Capel Curig road to the Pen-Gwryd hotel and the road up to Llanberis Pass, cars parked everywhere and *Car Park Full* signs at the top. Down the other side. Dinas Cromlech, castle-like on one side and the crags of Dinas Mot on the other. A glimpse of the sea. Starting to cloud over and spot with rain.

Llanberis on a wet weekday morning didn't seem like much of a tourist magnet. The mountain railway terminal was closed. Usually it was packed with overweight punters taking the easiest possible route to the top of Snowdon—the one where you paid your money and sat on your arse. Martin had to remind himself that there were plenty of people with physical disabilities who couldn't manage the climb and for whom the train ride was the only way up. *Don't sneer ...*

The main street was almost deserted. The wind filled out discarded carrier bags like balloons and kept them in the air for a few moments before they deflated and were whipped away.

A wave of depression washed over him. Llanberis in the rain. He drove up to the slate quarries and parked by the Bus Stop quarry. The cloud was low over the hills, the rain easing off a little. He put on his jacket and walked along the track to the Watford Gap. The hillsides gleamed with wet slate waste. He walked past the surreal landscape of Dali's Hole, the dead trees sticking out of water a curious shade of blue. They'd made a film up here recently. *Lord of the Rings?* No, that had been filmed in New Zealand. A film set in a post-nuclear holocaust wasteland would've been more appropriate.

He walked through the narrow defile of Watford Gap, vertical slate walls rising on either side. The valley above Llanber_s led up to the pass. The mountains towered above. He clambered over a fence and, slipping slightly on the wet slate underfoot, walked to the edge of the big hole of Twll Mawr. A raven rose and flapped away, its honks echoing from the walls.

He stood for a long time on a wile-coyote-style ledge, thinking about the meeting with his daughter; how she obviously blamed him for Julie's condition. One step and you'd launch yourself into a three-hundred-foot deep void.

He retraced his steps to the car park and checked his phone. Another text from Lester. Martin replied: *Still knackered. Maybe tomorrow?*

He drove down to Llanberis and parked on the main street—no problem finding a space today—and, buttoning up his jacket, headed for the nearest climbing shop. He startled the assistant, who was deeply engrossed in a James Paterson novel. The pasty-faced youth looked like he'd just received some terrible news, and his grey complexion could've done with a good dose of sunlight. So much for the great outdoors.

'Hi,' Martin said as warmly as he could. 'I was looking for an old climbing mate of mine. Haven't seen him for a few years. I heard he was working as an instructor round here. With Snowdonia Guides. Ben Hammond? He's most likely gone bald or something.'

'Ben Hammond? Don't know anyone ... Oh ...' The youth's morose face broke into a smile. 'You mean Bluto!'

'Bluto?'

'Yeah, you know. Popeye the sailor man? Big bastard with a bushy black beard. He's definitely not gone bald.' The youth checked his watch. 'He usually has his dinner in Pete's Eats. He should be there now.' He smiled as Martin turned to go. 'We've got some great offers on ropes ...'

Martin opened the door and a gust of wind whipped through the shop, drowning out the boy's voice.

Ben Hammond sat in a corner by himself, tucking with obvious relish into a plate piled high with chips, fried eggs, sausages and various other packages of fat and cholesterol. Martin would've put his appearance closer to Brian Blessed than Bluto. He collected a black coffee from the counter and approached Bluto/Blessed.

'Ben Hammond?' Martin said.

'Who wants to know?' Hammond's voice was high-pitched and with a scouse accent, not a deep bass like Blessed's as Martin had expected.

'Sorry.' Martin held out his hand. 'I'm an old friend of John Hardin's. I understand you were his colleague.'

Hammond put down his fork and shook Martin's hand. His limp handshake was a disappointment. Martin sat down in a chair on the opposite side of the small table.

'Right,' Hammond said. 'I was going to go to the funeral, but it was all over before I could find out about it. What was that all about?'

Martin stared into the other man's earnest face. Was he faking it?

'Look,' Martin said. 'I met him outside the Liverpool

Royal hospital. I'd not seen him for years, and then he collapsed on the escalator. I know it sounds crazy, but I think he was murdered. I'm trying to find out why.'

'Murdered!' Hammond's lips stretched back from his gums as he pronounced the word in a high falsetto. 'So are you with the busies or what?'

'They think it was a natural death. I'm afraid John was mixed up in some murky stuff in Liverpool. Drugs, that kind of thing. I was wondering if you knew anything about it.'

Hammond observed him for a moment. Then he laughed, a brittle laugh. 'Look, mate, you can't just walk in here while I'm having my dinner and accuse me of being involved in drug-pushing.' He attacked a rubbery sausage with his knife and fork. It resisted all his attempts to cut a piece off.

'I'm not accusing you of anything. You worked with John as a climbing instructor, didn't you?'

'That I did. For a couple of years. He was down on his luck. Needed a job. I climbed with him a bit back in the old days, when he was a superstar.' He paused. 'So how was he murdered?'

'He was injected on an escalator in the hospital. Something that made it look as if he'd had a heart attack.'

Hammond narrowed his eyes at him. 'You're joking,' he said. 'And the busies believe it was natural causes? How do I know you're not a nutcase?'

'I suppose you don't. But I know what I saw.'

Hammond concentrated on his sausage. This time he managed to pierce the tough outer skin and saw through it until his knife squeaked on the plate. He popped the piece of sausage into his mouth and looked at Martin, chewing hard. 'I'm sorry, I can't help you, mate.'

Martin turned away at the glimpse of masticated sausage.

'Look,' Hammond said, 'he was an old friend who'd hit hard times. He might've smoked a bit of weed, but I don't think he was into the hard stuff. He slept on my floor for two years. I would've known. Now, if you don't mind, I've got to do some shopping.'

Martin nodded and left the cafe. He waited in the car—well up the street where he hoped he wouldn't be noticed. After a few minutes, Hammond came out of the cafe and strolled along the street. He wore bright red and yellow climbing boots—gear for the mountain, not the street. He walked for a few yards, then got into a clapped-out-looking old red Fiesta. The indicator light came on. Martin started up, pulled out and followed the Fiesta for about a hundred yards until it turned and parked in front of a small Spar supermarket. Hammond got a shopping bag—one of the reusable ones everyone carried in their car now—from the boot and went in. Ten minutes later he came out with the bag full and obviously heavy.

Martin followed the Fiesta back to Betwys. Three miles further on it turned onto the Ffestiniog road.

Beyond the old slate-mining village of Penmachno, the narrow road led up into the remote cwym of Glasgym. Martin had to stay well back and lost sight of the Fiesta a few times, but he always managed to catch up. He had to be careful not to get too close. At the end of the tarmac road, the Fiesta turned off up a bumpy track. This wouldn't do the suspension any favours.

The track wound up through conifer plantations for what seemed like miles. Martin let the Fiesta get well ahead before he pulled out onto the edge of a ridge from which he could see a hillside that led down to a river.

The Fiesta was parked in front of a farmhouse. Smoke rose from the chimney. Someone was there. Martin parked his car up a rough forest road, out of sight of the track. He walked back to where he could see the farmhouse, sat down on a large tree trunk and waited.

After five minutes or so, Hammond came out of the farmhouse, got into the Fiesta, turned it round and came back up the rough track, driving too fast. The car bumped up and down and occasionally went airborne. Martin stepped back into the trees until the car went past, then he walked down to the farmhouse and tapped on the front door.

Silence. He went in. Empty. But a fire burned in the grate, and a half-drunk mug of coffee stood on the table. He touched it. Still warm. Someone obviously lived there. He went into the small kitchen and found fresh food in the fridge.

He did a quick search and uncovered a rusty, old-fashioned trunk under the bed. It contained books and documents. He found a name: John Hardin. So he'd lived here. A hideout in the mountains? He rummaged deeper and uncovered a photo album. He flipped through photos of Gayle. looking radiant on her wedding day, and John, Lester and Martin with long hair and all in suits:

wide lapels, bell bottoms, platform soles, kipper ties. Several pages showed a girl at varying ages. A blonde girl. His daughter. He stared for a long time at the last photo, of a fourteen-year-old Debbie, looking beautiful but slightly awkward.

On the way back to the main road, a farmer in denim overalls who stood in front of a battered Land Rover flagged him down.

'Sorry to bother you, sir.' The accent was thick north Welsh. 'But have you noticed anything suspicious? Wagons where they shouldn't be, things like that?'

Martin thought. 'No,' he said. 'What's going on?'

'It's sheep rustling.' The man grinned at Martin's expression. 'I know the jokes about the Welsh and sheep, but this is serious. They drive a livestock wagon up to a field gate. Rattle a spade in a metal bath. The sheep think it's scoff time, and before you know it the wagon's full. They slaughter them and send the meat to Ireland. The paddies re-export it as top quality lamb. Easy money. According to the police, the suspect vehicle is painted red and white. The plates are false and changed regularly.' He went back to the Land Rover and opened the driver's door. 'Keep an eye out, will you?'

CHAPTER EIGHTEEN

Jane did the obvious thing first and tried to access Whitaker's files from her own machine. She hoped there was no way they could check if someone was trying to do this.

The machine asked for the password.

She leaned back in her chair and surveyed the busy, open-plan office. Phones rang everywhere; people shouted into them and to people on the other side of the room. The mayor's embryonic support team had been shoved into a corner of the Hatton Gardens office—which stood two hundred yards from the Municipal Annexe, where Whitaker had his palatial office suite on the top floor, guarded by a stern, middle-aged secretary, Miss Dodd. The Hatton Gardens office, built in the Sixties' brutalist style, was a high-rise plastic and glass box with completely out-dated and worn-out interior fittings. Most likely the original fittings.

Rumour said it was about to be sold to be completely refurbished—down to the steel frame—for yuppie flats, so nothing was spent on maintenance. Take the toilets: seats were missing; doors hung on one hinge without locks; water—well, she hoped it was water—leaked everywhere so that the plastic floor tiles swelled and rose, tripping you up. Windows in the office couldn't be opened. People often tried, but they seemed to be glued shut. Once someone had brought in a jemmy, but no, they couldn't be budged.

She rang Miss Dodd. No reply. Out of the office? In the toilet? Jane pulled on her coat. Ann Smith had her head in a file. God knows what she was doing with it. The files were in a total mess, and when Jane tried to introduce a system, the woman met her idea with dumb insolence.

'Just nipping out for a sandwich,' she said to young Charlie, another so-called admin support officer. The whole team was paid for, like Jane herself, from an underspend on European Union financed regeneration programmes. Unfortunately, the team was made up of deadbeats, misfits and no-hopers—sent over from their original departments until they could be made redundant or pensioned off. The money was good, but her contract was only for two years. She was nine months in with an annual assessment due at the end of the year. She was dreading it.

Outside, a sunny but breezy day greeted her. The Municipal Annexe—a Victorian sandstone, former Conservative club in the French renaissance style—was only a short walk along Dale Street. It was grand enough to be a reasonable town hall for a mid-sized Lancashire mill town. Victorian Liverpool had overflowed with booty from the slave, rum and sugar trade, and they had to spend the surplus cash somewhere.

She took the stairs two at a time at first but slowed

down by the time she reached the top landing. She walked down the corridor to the door leading to Whitaker's office and was about to tap on it when she heard a phone ring and a click when someone picked it up. A female voice answered the call.

Jane strode back down the stairs, out onto Dale Street and towards the river. The yellow-brown water heaved and surged where the freshwater flow of the Mersey met an incoming tide in a display of incredible power, as if it were the Amazon or the Congo in flood. Was this the result of global warming? She felt faint and had to grab a rail. She closed her eyes and breathed as deeply as she could until she'd recovered.

A few minutes later, she walked back up Dale Street, into the annexe and up the stairs. She paused at the office door and knocked. This time there was no answer. She opened the door and stepped inside.

Miss Dodd's chair was empty. She walked over and tried Whitaker's door. Locked. She sat down at Miss Dodd's desk—a big, heavy, old-fashioned affair, and clear apart from the phone, computer and desk tidy. She tried the drawers. The second one contained an A4 diary as heavy and as thick as a substantial hardback book. She leafed through: meetings, meetings, meetings. On the last page she found a list of contact names and numbers with *peoplesteam1* halfway down. Whitaker was a keen Everton supporter, or bluebelly as Charlie, a confirmed red, called them.

Footsteps sounded on the tiles in the corridor outside. Jane put the diary back in the drawer, closed it and slipped down until the desk hid her. How could she explain this?

The door opened.

'Okay, okay,' Miss Dodd said into a mobile. 'Just hang on while I check in his office.'

Jane heard a key turning in a lock, followed by the low sound of Miss Dodd talking into her mobile in Whitaker's office. She took her chance to escape.

*

Barry Poole looked tired—deeply-lined face, bags under the eyes. He was easing into retirement and looked about ready for it. 'Could I have a word with you, Jane?' he said. 'I've got a bit of a problem.'

He made them a cup of coffee each and led the way into a small office in a corner of the big, open-plan office.

'How's it going?' he asked.

She shrugged. 'Not easy. Pressure from above.'

'From our glorious mayor?'

She nodded. 'And it's difficult knocking a support team into shape when it's one you didn't choose in the first place and is more like a drag team.'

'What, like wigs, false eyelashes and falsies?'

'No.' She smiled. 'More like the opposite of support.'

'The trouble is,' he said, 'things are changing too quickly round here. The people who can get out have gone, and the people who can't escape make up your support team. Austerity and technological change. Computers have made typing pools redundant. Remember when they used carbons and Tippex? Now you change it on the screen, save it and print it off. There used to be print rooms and armies of technicians; now an architect uses CAD and prints the plans off.'

'Have you been to a seminar on this subject recently?'

'As a matter of fact, I have. It was organised by the HR Department.' He looked at her. 'Listen, Jane. I've got a problem with one of your team.'

She sighed.

'Ann Smith,' he said. 'According to the building supervisor, she's here when he comes in at seven in the morning, and she's still there at night when he leaves at eight. It's a health and safety issue. Suppose she got attacked and raped? Could you look into it for me?'

Jane had noticed that Ann racked up enormous flex-time backlogs but never took a day off. Once she'd read Ann's personal file. It'd been about three inches thick, stuffed with sick notes, most likely a story of divorce and bad luck.

She sighed. 'Okay. I'll look into it. But it's just another example of drag team rather than support team.'

*

The veterinary hospital looked new. A single-storey building with pink sandstone cladding. Bruce knew something was up and wouldn't get out of the car. Jane had to order him out.

Yellow pine inside. Clean and modern. A middle-aged, overweight man in a tracksuit and scruffy trainers stood at the counter; his springer spaniel sat patiently at his side. A German shepherd sprawled at the feet of a lady sitting in one of the chairs. Bruce pulled on the lead to try and investigate the other dogs and make friends. Typical golden retriever. Jane made him stand at heel.

An assistant weighed Bruce. Thirty-eight kilos. Normal. They had to sit for a few minutes before being called in. A young female vet with a blue smock over ordinary clothes gave her the results of the tests. Bruce had a mast-cell tumour at the base of his tail.

'It'll have to come off,' the girl said.

Jane glanced at her and then at Bruce. 'What'll have to come off?'

'His tail. It's the only way. Otherwise it could spread.' The girl waited patiently. 'You'll have to leave him and collect him tomorrow.'

This was difficult. How could she look after him? Whitaker had already left two messages on her mobile, wanting to know where she was and how she was getting on with the strategy—micro-managing as usual. With most bosses you could talk a problem over with them, but he might say no, and she had no alternatives.

She put in a lot more hours and energy into the job than her contract stipulated, but he didn't seem to recognise that.

*

Jane turned the chicken pieces in the frying pan and wrinkled her nose in disgust. She might be vegetarian, but Bruce loved chicken. She'd keep half of it in the fridge for when she brought him home after the operation. A treat. He'd be sore and disorientated, shaved and stitched up like a chicken ready for the oven. She looked out the window. It was getting dark. A planet, Venus most probably, stood out over the trees. It'd seemed like a good idea, renting a three-bedroom, semi-detached house on the edge of the suburbs, next to a big park and only a ten-minute walk from the station one way and five minutes to the shops the other. Nice and quiet. Too quiet at times. Her mobile buzzed on the worktop. Most likely Whitaker again. She had no holidays left. She'd have to call in sick. She hated doing it, but it was the only way. She'd look at the strategy tonight and compose a reply for him.

Getting Whitaker's password had proved to be a disappointment. She couldn't find anything remotely incriminating. His e-mail record had big gaps, and the filing system was perfunctory. Whitaker had probably permanently deleted anything remotely dodgy. The police might be able to retrieve the deleted stuff, but only with a court order. Which wasn't on. It was a dead end.

The phone stopped buzzing. She turned the cooker ring off and opened the mobile. Yep, two messages from Whitaker. No point answering—it would just be more harassment about some project or other. And one from a number she didn't recognise. She listened and immediately knew who it was. A chill ran down her back.

'Hi, darling. See you soon. Love, Steve'.

CHAPTER NINETEEN

'Okay, Mr Hughes.' Brenda looked through the checklist on her knee. 'We'll put the company history on hold for a moment. I know it doesn't sound important, but these days banks are paranoid about anything untoward.' She paused. 'Before we get to the cash flows, let's have a look at the SWOT analysis again. I know they're a pain, but you've got to do them.'

Jimmy couldn't see what she was getting at. Cash flows were the best bit.

She pulled out a sheet of paper and scanned it. 'I see you've done some market research.'

Brenda Pullman couldn't have looked less like a financial adviser. Short, fat and with what looked like a cross between a tea cosy and a wig on her head. Yet she was clever. She would see through any inconsistencies in the story. Jimmy was stuck. He'd blagged over the company history, referring to its origins in a rough environment of construction and security. In the Eighties, Liverpool overflowed with dodgy companies dealing in cash. That had all changed, of course. Mersey Estates was as law-abiding as you could get.

Jimmy turned and stared out of the picture window at the back garden. You had to stand on tiptoes in the front bedroom to see the sea, but when you went outside you could taste the salt in the air. The manicured lawn with flower beds on each side ran down to a fence and a copse of trees. This was a nice house in one of the choicer locations in Southport, and he would do everything in his power to keep it.

He turned. She had her head down, shuffling papers. Did she suspect anything? Probably not. She was no doubt used to rough-arsed builders and the like trying to move upmarket. The important thing was to avoid any link whatsoever with Mick Malone and his activities.

'This is all good stuff,' she said. 'It can go in the opportunities section. The bank likes to see evidence that you've got up off your backside and done some research.' She scanned through. 'Strengths: Northern Powerhouse, improved road and rail connections—but some way off; new bridge under construction, though. And the opportunities: 52,000 students, many from overseas, who often invest in the area in future, for example, by buying to-let properties; some big developments like Shop Direct; demand for high-end properties—footballers' flats and mansions—in Southport, the Wirral and on the waterfront. Weaknesses: downturn in house values of twenty percent; full scale recovery some way off. I like the historical context: long term depopulation, about halved from 1931 to 2011. But this section on threats is a bit thin. Nowadays everyone puts in a bit about the recession and the downturn. You don't seem to be worried about the competition, do you?'

She went back to shuffling the papers.

Jimmy almost smiled but stopped himself. The competition hadn't had access to endless amounts of free cash. He had a good team. He could whup the competition's ass on service and quality. No, the main threat was not something you could put in a business plan.

The irony was that, in the good old days, if there'd been a threat to the operation, Harry and Chucky would've got someone like Malone to sort it out, by any means necessary. Now Jimmy had to sort out Malone but without access to the violent means and before the idiot got arrested for some stupid murder or botched deal and attracted the attention of the plods. There was no need now for any link between the two operations. Mersey Estates was a standalone. Time to cut the rope. It would be worth the risk.

But he wouldn't know where to start with sorting Malone out. There again, that might be an advantage. Malone obviously felt contempt for him. He wouldn't be expecting any rough stuff. The question was, how to do it? It would have to be something subtle, something Malone wouldn't expect. An accident? Maybe in the old Pools building. You could hide a body there, no problem. Rubbish and rubble everywhere. Might be a risk of being seen by kids or some rough sleeper, though. But he wasn't a gangster, not a hard man. He was a mild-mannered surveyor who wouldn't say boo to a goose. That was the truth. Was he up to the task of getting rid of Malone with all the risk that involved?

He thought for a while and had an idea. The problem with the conversion to residential flats proposal for the

Pools building was that there wasn't much space for gardens or car parking. But students wouldn't be arsed with gardening, and these days not many could afford cars. And, anyway, it was within walking distance of the universities. There was a big demand for student flats. This could be the big project the business plan needed. And it would get rid of a white elephant. Two birds with one stone. He would get the architect to draw up some plans tomorrow.

'Mr Hughes?' she said.

He looked up.

She was watching him. 'Threats?'

*

'Where do I see UKIP in five years' time? In power, of course. Or at least in coalition.'

James Whitaker turned from staring at the Liverpool skyline. What a panorama: Liver Buildings, Albert Dock, Wheel, cathedral. One of the best views in the city, and from his own office.

Justin Smith certainly looked the part of a spin doctor: too young; too well-dressed; too cocky; a bit like a younger version of himself, but not as smart—a balloonhead.

'Exactly,' Smith said, 'but we're not going to do it without a complete rethink, are we? Let's start with the name. UKIP. UK Independence Party. A one-trick pony. Once we won the EU vote we had nowhere to go. What's the composition of our appeal to the average voter?'

Whitaker laughed. 'I heard a story,' he said, 'that

when you realised that you had no actual policies, you noted down the *Daily Mail* headlines and sent out people with notebooks to sit in pubs and jot down what drunken gobshites were saying.'

'Totally cynical, but not far from the truth. We need a complete makeover, and we need a proper policy agenda that will appeal to our target voter. Opportunism and populism aren't enough ...'

'I've done well enough out of them,' Whitaker said.

'Exactly. That's why we're courting you. You know how to tap into what the average pub gobshite is saying.'

'I've got no illusions about the secret of my appeal, mate. But don't forget that there's a core of integrity in how I operate. I try and help ordinary working people. I build houses, create jobs, keep the rates down.'

'Exactly.' Smith nodded. 'I agree with everything you're saying, but we need to be more right wing than the Tories. Cut back the state. Give power back to the man in the street. Have you read Ayn Rand?'

'Isn't she the Nazi nutcase who said the poor should be left to starve in the streets? And that American politician, Rand Paul, isn't he named after her? He's a nutcase too, isn't he?'

'That's just leftie propaganda.' Smith produced a paperback book and handed it over. The lady on the front was smoking a ciggy. She looked like Lauren Bacall, but not as sexy, and had a strange resemblance to his own dear wife, who'd just served divorce papers, bless her. This broad certainly looked as hard.

'Read this and tell me what you think,' Smith said.

'And google Rand Paul. Okay, each of them is a bit nutty at times, but there's a lot of stuff we can use.'

Whitaker stared at the book cover. 'I like the cigarette. That was a winner for Nigel, wasn't it? Along with the pint. Why should do-gooding nannies stop you having a bit of pleasure? Not that I agree with smoking myself.' He thought. 'Ayn Rand. Isn't she the one who was against national health services, but when she was dying of cancer she took advantage of a public hospital?'

'Another bit of leftie propaganda. Her idea was to encourage people to fend for themselves rather than rely on the state.'

Whitaker wondered if there was a way to murder someone and make it look like they'd died of cancer. No, you had to have a tumour or something. Poison might be a way, but they were hot on that kind of thing nowadays. What was it they used in *Breaking Bad*? Risin. But you'd need to be a chemical genius to use that and get away with it. It was easy for some fucking screenwriter to google *risin* and then make the main character a chemical genius, but you'd never get away with it in real life, and if you had the highest political ambitions then you couldn't take a risk like that.

Smith put on a serious face. 'What about skeletons in the cupboard?'

'What?'

'I've got to ask you this. We've had so many problems recently with lunatics and chancers joining the party and bringing baggage with them. One feller had served a sentence for throwing a hand grenade into a synagogue.' He paused and smiled. 'Not that I'm calling you a lunatic or a chancer, of course.' He laughed. 'I know you're happily married—Pamela's a lovely woman—but I've got to ask you this: is there any baggage? Shags or hags? People who might seek revenge? If there's anything there, the press will tease it out and save it up for the worst possible moment. And the so-called right wing press are the worst.'

Whitaker considered the matter. Pamela was the perfect political wife. She was hard work, but it would take time to replace her. He had to keep her on board. There were loads of shags, of course, but nothing that might come back to haunt him. A few shags might even make him look like a bit of a lad and attract the gullible female vote. No, probably nothing to worry about there. But there was the connection in the early days when he'd run the agency and been threatened if he didn't turn a blind eye to the money laundering and the scams. All kinds of people had been involved, from lawyers and councillors to big Chewbacca lookalikes. Chuckie was away for life and Wacker was dead. Whitaker had even based his mayoral campaign on fighting organised crime in the city. But someone might sing about it all in return for a mittful of silver. A clean-up might be called for. And as soon as possible.

'Look,' Smith said. 'I'll get down to the nub of it. What we need is someone to take our housing policy forward. Take a look at the green belt policies and housing demand. We need a coherent argument to answer the NIMBYs and the tree-huggers. Why separate town and country? It used to be the toffs trying to stop the proles spilling over into the countryside. The greatest irony is that the Marxists—Engels and Trotsky—tried to abolish the division between town and country. You can't get more left wing than Trotsky, can you?'

He laughed before continuing. 'So by getting rid of the green belt we'd be striking a massive blow for social justice. Give the people what they want, James. Bring house prices down. Vote winner or what?'

*

'Darling! How nice to hear from you!'

Pamela sounded cordial and haughty—a very bad sign. Her nickname with her friends was 'Lady Pamela', and under no circumstances would she answer to 'Pam'. She spoke to him exactly like a lady from *Downton Abbey* reproaching a servant for a minor misdemeanour. Whitaker took several deep breaths. *Don't let her wind you up.*

'Hi, love,' he said. 'I was wondering if you fancied dinner tonight. We could try that new place in Liverpool One. You know, the one that's been in the news. We could do the old loving couple thing.'

'I'd love to, pet, but I'm busy, like you must've been this afternoon.'

Oh shit. 'Look, I'm sorry, something came up …'

'Never mind, sweet; it was obviously more important than your son's swimming lesson.'

'Pamela, I—'

'You'll be turning up tomorrow night, of course.'

'Tomorrow night? I've got something important—'

'Don't tell me you've forgotten it's your daughter's birthday. Shagging the latest slut, are you?'

Shit! But he had to sort out the skeleton in the cupboard. 'Look, Pamela, I'll do anything to—'

'The only thing I want you to do, darling, is sign the divorce papers.'

His stomach churned, and sweat broke out on his brow. Her tone was so calm and collected as if she were sending a servant on an errand. God, he could kill her, throttle her. He could feel his hands tightening around the smooth skin of her throat, see the beautiful green eye balls popping out of their sockets.

But no.

'Pamela, I can't do that. You know that. I need...'

'You need me to further your nasty little political ambitions.'

'Pamela, I'll do anything ...'

'Anything?'

He listened to her list of demands. She drove a hard bargain, especially on the question of the increase in maintenance—inflation, increased school fees, blah-de-blah. But there was nothing that wasn't doable.

CHAPTER TWENTY

'Aw, fuckin' hell!' A squeaky, high-pitched voice cut through the sounds of a busy pub. 'Not him again, the useless git!'

The Old Police Station pub was always busy on match days. When it got close to kick-off, they often locked the doors. Martin usually avoided it at such times as it was filled to overflowing, including several gangs of raucous drunks who'd been at it all day.

This afternoon, he was just in time, though it took him ten minutes to get served in the crush, despite there being twice the usual number of bar staff, all working like mad. The volume on the tellies was turned up to the maximum as the commentator got excited about the coming match. Combined with a hundred shouted conversations, it made it difficult to even think.

Martin edged closer to the source of the voice.

'Hey, Mick!' someone shouted. 'What're yer having!'

Martin squeezed between two drinkers whose beer bellies met and formed an almost impassable barrier.

A man in his forties with a ridiculous spiky mullet hairstyle held up a glass and shouted to someone at the bar. 'Pint of Stella, lar!'

That high-pitched, squeaky voice belonged to one of

the characters who'd searched John's flat. Mullet-man turned to a man standing next to him. The brute was so big that he had to bend down to hear.

'Why do they keep playing that feller, Gobby?' said the man with the mullet, his voice like a rusty door hinge. 'He can't fuckin' defend, and he always loses the ball in his own half trying to dribble like George Best.'

His mate grunted in reply. Martin made a mental note: Mick Malone and Gobby Gilbert. The pair from John's flat.

The match started and the hub-bub died down a little. As usual with a home match at Anfield, the Liverpool side attacked in a frenzy from the whistle, and the away side defended desperately. Martin drained his glass and managed to get to the bar without too much trouble as everyone was intent on watching the match. He got back to his original position and leaned against the wall, sipping his pint and watching the match for a few minutes. The fullback charged down the wing.

'On yer bike, lar!' shouted someone in the crowd.

'Oh no!' Malone shouted. 'He thinks he's fuckin' George Best again. Get back to where you're supposed to be, knobhead—defending!'

Martin edged closer until he stood by Malone's side. Malone's mobile went off and he edged towards the door, which led out to a small beer garden—really just a couple of picnic benches in a concreted yard. Martin followed him until he was inside the doorway, where he could just about hear the phone conversation without being seen.

'A'right there, Benny lad!' Malone shouted into the

phone. Martin didn't catch the rest of the conversation. Just a brief mumbled sentence: 'Yeh, all right.' Then the pitch of Malone's voice changed. The conversation was about to end.

Martin moved back to his previous position just as Malone came in the door.

On the telly, the fullback feinted, then cut inside the opposition fullback before unleashing a terrific shot from twenty-five yards that rocketed into the far top corner of the net with the goalie clawing at the air.

The pub erupted.

Malone half turned and leapt in the air. 'What a goal, eh!' he yelled. 'I always said that feller was a great player!'

Martin left.

*

Martin walked down the main street, taking in the spicy smells drifting from the Indian takeaway. He stopped at the corner and listened. Screams and shouts came from somewhere nearby. Whitney Houston? No, she was a wailer and a shrieker. This was someone in pain. A man's voice. Sounded like someone was being hacked to death with a blunt machete. Martin was used to such things here. It was usually teenaged girls who screamed as their male companions messed about. And if they really were being attacked and raped?

He walked to the front door, put the key in the lock and stopped. The sound was much louder now. It came from inside, from upstairs. He took the stairs two at a time, flung open the door to the back bedroom and switched on the light.

Two big, meaty hands were stuck in the bottom of the sash, the bloated fingers digging in to the sill. Martin ran forward and gripped the sash. He could see a big face through the glass, its features contorted with pain.

'Help me!' the man screamed.

Martin stepped back. Who was this man? He could be a burglar or a thug sent by gangsters to work him over. He ran downstairs and into the kitchen, and found a hammer and a roll of duct tape. Back upstairs, he approached the window slowly.

'Come on!' yelled the man, his voice muffled by the glass. 'I can't stand much more of this!'

'Who are you?' Martin asked.

'What? I'm Ronnie Ryan, the nurse from the hospital where your wife was. Remember?'

'Why are you here?'

No reply.

'You were breaking in, weren't you?' Martin said. 'I think I'll call the police.'

'No, please, get this window off my hands and I'll explain everything.'

Martin tried to lift the sash. It wouldn't budge. Jammed. He wedged the claw of the hammer in and wrenched upwards. The sash moved slightly, and he managed to lift it up. The man climbed in and rolled on the floor. He looked up at Martin standing with the hammer.

'Put that away. My hands are fucked. Look.' He held out his hands. They looked ridiculously flattened, exactly like in the childhood incident when Martin had got his own hands caught in a sash window. Ryan half rolled, half stumbled to the room's armchair. 'Look,' he said. 'I need something cold. Have you got any packs of frozen peas, something like that?'

Martin picked up the duct tape, ran forward, pushed the man back into the chair and unrolled the duct tape around his chest and the back of the armchair until he was secured.

'Fuck off!' the man groaned. 'You stupid twat, I can't hurt you in this condition!'

Martin couldn't find any peas in the freezer, just green beans and broad beans. Back upstairs, he got the man to put his hands forward and he put a pack on each hand.

'Ah!' the man moaned.

Martin sat down on a chair opposite, the hammer in his hand. 'Right,' he said. 'We'll start with your name.'

The man laughed. 'I've already told you once. Are you stupid or deaf? Ryan. Ronnie Ryan. I've heard all about you from Julie.'

'What have you heard?'

'Never you mind what I've heard. Why have you been harassing her?'

Martin leaned forward, lifted the pack of broad beans and gripped the hand.

Ryan screamed.

'What has she told you?'

'That you're responsible for her condition. With your behaviour. Running around with other women and abandoning your family to go climbing.'

'Right. So I'm the bastard. Now we've got that clear, why are you here? You were going to give me a good hiding, weren't you? Teach me a lesson.'

Ryan said nothing.

Martin sat back in the chair and let him think things over for a while.

'Look,' Ryan said at last. 'I love Julie. I think she can recover from her problems, enough to live a normal life outside.'

'I honestly wish you the best of luck,' Martin said. 'If you manage it, you're a better man than I am.'

'Yeah, well, you were responsible for her problems, weren't you?'

'There's always two sides to something like this,' Martin said, then he fell silent for a few moments. 'Let me tell you the truth,' he went on. 'I admit that I behaved badly, but like in all these things, it's six of one, half a dozen of the other. Could I tell you what really happened?' He stopped talking and formed the question with his expression.

Ryan shrugged.

The desire to tell someone, anyone, took hold of Martin, and there was nothing he could do about it. 'I went to work one day and forgot to take in a report I'd been working on at home. I needed it for an important meeting, so I came back. I was on the stairs when I heard something strange going on in the bathroom. I walked up to the door and listened. The shower was going. All I could hear was this strange squelching, slapping sound with the shower going in the background. Then someone moaned: 'I love you, John. I love you, John. I've always loved you.' It was Julie, my wife. She was fucking my best friend, John Hardin, in the shower.'

Ryan just stared at him.

Martin looked away and swallowed. 'She would never have done that or talked like that with me.' Admitting this was highly embarrassing, but once he'd got started he couldn't stop it gushing out. 'So John wasn't just a better climber than me, he was a better lover. I went quietly downstairs and never said a word about it to either of them, but it'd sunk a poisoned dart into my heart, mate. We were never the same again. Our daughter came along, and I loved her, but the marriage was never the same.' His face must be bright red from embarrassment. 'I met John Hardin again recently. He was murdered on an escalator in the Royal ...'

'Murdered? Come on.'

'Yes, murdered. He was mixed up in something illegal. Something bad to do with drugs.' Martin paused. Should he mention finding Julie's number on John's iPad? No. 'He was cremated quickly,' he continued. 'Too quickly. There's something going on. This bent solicitor, Benny Carter, was involved ...'

'Benny Carter? The one who represents the footballers?'

'That's the one. The doctor signed off the cremation, then disappeared.'

'What was the name of this doctor?'

'Angelo. From the Philippines. He's gone back there.'

'I worked in the Royal for a few years. Still got contacts there. There's a set procedure for signing off deaths.

If what you're saying is true, then there is something fishy going on.' He held out his hands, a bag of frozen green beans on one and a bag of broad beans on the other. 'I couldn't punch my way out of a wet paper bag with these hands,' he said. 'Never mind work you over. I don't think they're broken, but even if they're not, it'll take a few days for the swelling to go down. Let's make a deal. I'll take you at your word and check up on this doctor if you'll let me go.'

CHAPTER TWENTY-ONE

The telephone ringing woke Martin the next morning. 'Martin? It's Ronnie.'

'Who?' Martin muttered, still half asleep. His throat caught on phlegm, and he went into a coughing fit. Those bloody pills.

'Ronnie Ryan. Julie's nurse. Remember? My hands hurt like hell. Look, I checked up on John Hardin for you.'

'Oh, yeah ..'

'You don't sound too good yourself.'

Martin glanced at the clock by his bed. Half nine. Shit, he'd slept in. 'Sorry,' he grunted. 'Go on.'

'There is something fishy going on. My contact at the hospital was cagey. It was all signed off very quickly. It's not usually that fast. They normally follow the rules carefully. Especially if the police and the coroner might be involved. Someone's taken a big risk to cover this up. And once the body's cremated, that's it. Any forensic evidence is gone. If I were you, I'd ask this Benny Carter what's going on.'

*

For a solicitor who acted for several well-known footballers, Benny Carter's offices were hardly prepossessing. Downright ordinary, they occupied much of the upper floor of a block of two-storey shops in a Liverpool suburb, right opposite the bus stop. Martin had decided that it wasn't worth the risk to use his car in the city, and taxis were too expensive for him at the moment.

The main entrance was via a ground-floor shop unit with the window fully occupied by a sign reading, *Had a Trip or a Crash? Contact Us for Cash!* He'd arrived a couple of minutes early for his eleven o'clock appointment. It'd been remarkably easy to get an immediate appointment with Benny Carter himself. He'd normally expect a junior solicitor to handle a straightforward job like this.

Inside, the decor was a bit more upmarket than the location: oak furniture, pastel shades and modern art prints on the walls. He didn't have to wait long and was soon being shown up the stairs by the receptionist, who was about eighteen—blonde and with long, long legs.

Benny Carter stood at the window, staring out. At what? Martin wondered. It was hardly a good view. Short, dark and bearded, Carter wore a surprisingly seedy pinstripe suit. Although receding, his longish hair bore the hint of a Beatle hairstyle, which put him in his sixties—not a good age to go to prison. Martin had done a bit of research via Google. Carter would be standing before a judge soon on charges of money laundering.

'Ah, Mr Bennett, have a seat.' Carter walked round to where two low, black-leather armchairs faced each other across a coffee table and motioned Martin to do the same.

The leather made a slight farting noise when Martin sat down.

'Right,' Carter said, checking his watch. 'How can I help you? I understand you had a trip on a paving slab?'

'Yep. Not far from here.'

'Where, exactly?'

'Outside the Aldi.'

Carter laughed. 'By the trolleys?'

'How did you know that?'

'Let's just say that that location is well-known locally. What happened?'

'I was walking past Aldi this morning when I tripped, landed hard and twisted something in my back. I've got a photo of the paving slab on my mobile phone with a pound coin next to it. The trip's at least an inch high. And the date and time are on the photo.'

'Excellent,' Carter said as he made some notes. 'A dated photo with a coin is important. The weather was good this morning. Have you seen a doctor?'

'Not yet.'

'Do it. As soon as you can. Emphasise the severity of the injury, and get time off work. I'll send a letter to the local council and send you a copy. I'll include a form; fill that in and send it back to me. Details, everything. That's important.'

'So what are the chances?'

'The council will deny responsibility, of course. They'll say that they've got a good system in place to inspect pavements on a regular basis. But I've done enough of these cases to challenge them. With a bit of luck, they'll settle out of court. You realise that this is no win, no fee?' He handed over a sheet of paper. 'Our rates are set out in these notes.'

'What might we get?'

'Anything from two K right up to a hundred K plus.'

Martin whistled. 'So what should I put that sort of money into? The building society is a waste of time with the rates you get at the moment. What about these high-yield investments? I heard that you can organise those.'

'Where did you hear that?'

Martin put on an innocent look and shrugged.

'I'm not involved in that kind of thing anymore.' Carter looked at his watch. 'Is there anything else I can help you with, Mr Bennett?'

Papers were scattered over the desk, and a pile of messages lay next to the phone. Martin managed to read the top one upside down: *Harry Fellows Freeway Investment Services* and a phone number. That rang a bell somewhere.

'I'm a friend of John Hardin,' Martin said. 'I understand you arranged his cremation. I was a little surprised at how quickly it was carried out.'

Carter looked like he'd been smacked in the face. 'Ah, well,' he said at last. 'The problem was the hospital couldn't find any relatives, or relatives who were willing to take responsibility, so I had to do it.'

'In what role were you acting for John?'

'Oh, a property transaction.'

A property transaction? In North Wales?

Carter leaned forward. 'This kind of thing happens quite often. Vagrants or people living alone die and there're no relatives, so the council pays for the funeral or cremation. Were you a good friend? I apologise for the unseemly haste, but in these cases it all happens very quickly.'

John hadn't been homeless; he'd been living in a flat, and he had step-parents who lived in St Helens. But before Martin had time to think of what else to say, he was being ushered down the stairs and out onto the street.

According to the timetable in the bus shelter, the next one wouldn't be along for ten minutes so he had a while to think things over.

Why had a big-time solicitor like Benny Carter taken it on himself to organise the cremation of a client who he hardly could've known very well? And what was the property transaction for which he'd been acting for John Hardin? He found a scrap of paper and a pen and wrote down *Harry Fellows Freeway Investment Services* and the phone number. He recognised the name now.

CHAPTER TWENTY-TWO

Steven Lightfoot couldn't believe his luck. Two birds with one stone. From where he sat in the layby he could see the client's house and also the junction of a cul-de-sac with the main road. The name looked familiar. He checked in his smartphone. Bingo! What was the word? Serendipity. He googled the word. 'The occurrence and development of events by chance in a happy or beneficial way.' That was exactly it. Serendipity.

Things were moving. His client came out of the house, got into the big white car parked in the drive and drove off. He started up the engine and followed her for half a mile to a Sainsburys car park.

He parked well away from his client's car, pulled on his fleece and put his baseball cap on—best to blend in and not draw attention to himself. When you were six feet tall and as well-muscled as he was, you tended to stand out in a crowd, drawing admiring glances from the ladies and jealous stares from the men.

He grabbed the shoulder bag from the passenger seat, got out of his van and locked the door. Time to tail the suspect on foot. The Sainsburys car park was quite busy at this time of day. Despite the time restriction, people obviously used it as a car park for the village.

He had to nail this one asap. There was only one thing worse than a bossy cow like Jane Trevelyan as your partner, and that was a bossy gobshite as your boss.

His client, Sheila Woodridge, was just going in the main entrance. He walked slowly—*don't get too close*—stopped at the entrance and looked back over the car park at his van, parked three bays down in the second row: an off-white, nearly new Transit Connect with *SLL Surveys* written on the side in black letters and a set of extendible ladders on the roof rack. SLL came from his own initials, Steven Leighton Lightfoot. It didn't say what kind of surveys. Drains? Trees? Buildings?

Empty Costa coffee cartons, KFC boxes and rolled up *Sun* and *Star* newspapers cluttered the dashboard, and one-way glass darkened the rear windows of the van. You couldn't see in, but you could see out. It was kitted out as a cosy little hideaway where he could watch and film whatever was going on. A yellow fluorescent jacket lay on the front passenger seat, just like any work van. You had to have a sense of humour in this game; without it you were buggered.

He grabbed a basket, went into the supermarket and put a pack of tuna salad sandwiches and a real orange drink into the basket—no pies or choccy bars. He prided himself on his twelve-stone, six-foot frame. What was it the kids called it? Ripped. You had two choices in life, athlete or slob, and he knew which choice he'd always make.

There she was, getting a tin from the top shelf for an old lady. He put the basket down and pressed the switch on the top of the video recorder in his bag. Sheila couldn't walk, drive or tie her own shoelaces. She had arthritis, heart problems, IBS and a prolapsed disc. That was what she'd told the Job Centre and the others. As she stretched up, her heavy breasts thrust against the material of her T-shirt under the track suit top, attracting the rude stare of a nearby elderly man. Steven chuckled quietly. Not bad. He wouldn't have minded giving her one himself, except that you had to have some professional standards.

He even felt a bit sorry for her. He had her bang to rights, but you had to harden your heart. She was a benefits scrounger living off his taxes. She would deserve everything she got.

He kept his distance, following her out to her car—a brand-new white BMW off roader. Worth what? Thirty grand? Not bad for someone on council tax benefit, income support, housing benefit and disability benefit.

He went to his own vehicle, got in, started up and followed her out of the car park. Within five minutes they were out in open country. He kept her just in sight all the way. Softly, softly, catchee monkey. He was well-practised at this game. They came to a motorway junction where she turned off up a road and then into a hotel car park, pulling up outside a gym. He parked at the other end of the car park, then leaned into the back for his own sports bag with his jogging gear.

He walked into the reception as Sheila went through the door to the changing rooms.

'Hi!' he said to the lady behind reception. She was in her forties, pretty, but quite heavily made up. Track suit. Nice figure. Mutton dressed as lamb, but not bad. Looked bored out of her skull. 'I'm interested in joining,' he said, 'but is it possible to have a quick look around to see if I like it? I've been told by the doctor to eat more healthily and get more exercise. Fight the flab.' He smiled at her and rubbed his tummy.

'Certainly, sir.' She smiled back and reached down for a form. 'Through that door over there. If you like it, come back here and we'll sort out a membership application. Just fill in this form. It's quite short.' She looked him up and down, taking in the muscles highlighted by the tight, white T-shirt. 'You don't look like you need much work.'

Steven grinned. 'There's one thing I've learned in life, love ...' He posed the question with his eyes.

'Sally.'

'If there's one thing I've learned in life, Sally, it's that if a job's worth doing, it's worth doing well. And you don't get any more out of life than what you put in.' That was two things but never mind, he'd caught her interest.

'That's very true. I wish you could get that message through to the people who come in here expecting to be size-eight gorgeous after two weeks.'

Steven followed her gaze over to a window where Sheila sat on an exercise bike. She hardly moved, more interested in watching something on the tablet set into the handlebars than on cycling.

He raised a questioning eyebrow at Sally, and she answered with a giggle.

After writing fictitious details on the form, he went in and got changed, then took the bag with the video recorder and strolled into the gym. Two overweight middle-aged women thumped away on the treadmills. He nodded and smiled when they looked him over, then went over to a bench, put the bag next to him and, pretending to look for something in it, switched on the recorder. A sign said *No bags allowed*, but there were no staff in sight. He pulled out the bottle of orange and took a swig. Sheila was now vigorously lifting heavy dumbbells. She put them down with a thump and stood, bent over, breathing hard. When she'd recovered she headed for the exercise bike.

Steven couldn't contain his excitement. This was fantastic stuff. Perfect. He moved the bag so the camera would include her, then moved it again when she went on the rowing machine and then onto a treadmill. Her breasts bounced up and down like two fat Labrador puppies in a sack.

Steven carefully avoided any eye contact. She looked like a nice woman, probably really accommodating, unlike the bossy cows he usually got stuck with. Mrs Jane droopy-drawers to name but one. You weren't supposed to mix business with pleasure, but sometimes business was a pleasure. Well, this was business finished for the day. Now for the real pleasure, and like any real pleasure it would involve risk—like getting caught and having to serve another custodial sentence.

He knew what she'd tell the cops, that he was a lying psychopath without a conscience. He'd had enough discussions with the shrinks inside and knew more than them about the condition. He could question his own behaviour and knew the difference between right and wrong. If he could honestly ask himself 'Is it me?' and the answer was 'no', then he wasn't crackers, he was sane. But the risk would be worth it. As the poet said, 'Revenge is a dish best served cold.' He'd checked out the cow's house, noted the dog; all it needed was a nice piece of fillet steak. No golden retriever worth its salt could resist that.

He switched the camera off, then popped into the toilet, where he examined himself in the mirror. Yes, he was a handsome hunk of a man, even though he said it himself. He looked round. The changing room was empty.

'I'm a handsome hunk of a man!' he yelled. The noise reverberated around the walls of the large, empty room and the toilets and showers that led off it. He listened. He might have startled someone sitting and having a quiet dump, but when you'd got it, baby, you might as well flaunt it. He listened. Silence, apart from some low music somewhere.

He found Sally sitting at a table in the coffee bar with a sandwich and coke. He bought a coffee and went over, his bag slung over his shoulder.

'Hi!' he said. 'Lunch break?'

She nodded and smiled. 'Have a seat.'

'If you don't mind me saying so, Sally, you look like you've spent some time in the gym yourself.'

She smiled. 'I like to keep in shape.' She showed him her sandwich: wholemeal bread, salad and cheese. 'This is as important as exercise.'

A loud braying sound came from behind them. Steve turned. Sheila sat at a table with a friend. She was leaning back and howling with laughter, a big slab of half-eaten cream cake in her hand.

'It's so sad.' Sally grinned. 'They mess about for an hour, not really exercising, then they come in here and fill up on whatever is most fattening.' She looked at him. 'Are you here on business?'

'Yeah,' he said. 'We're about to pull off a big deal. What's it like staying here?' It wouldn't be cheap, but he was on expenses.

She was concentrating on finishing her sandwich. 'Basic, but okay.'

'Well ...' he said. Faint heart never won fair lady.

CHAPTER TWENTY-THREE

Martin leafed through the Yellow Pages until he came to *Freeway Investment Services*. He tried the number and got an answerphone with a female voice. He switched on the computer, googled *Companies House* and ran a Webcheck: Freeway Investment Services Ltd. Registered office Unit 5, Freeway Business Park. He knew it. Next to the Freeway Centre—the retail park. Nature of business: investment advice, importing and exporting. Sole director Harold Fellows.

He leaned back in his chair and took a sip of coffee. Harold Fellows. Harry Fellows. Councillor Harry Fellows. A key member of the committee that had sacked him. Someone whom Martin was sure knew more than he was letting on. He checked the local council website. Harry Fellows was no longer a councillor. He googled the name and came up with page after page of hits. Harry Fellows and Freeway Investment Services were under investigation by the Financial Control Authority. He'd taken money off punters to invest in pension plans but instead had used it to fund his own business activities of importing and exporting food and drink. Benny Carter's name was frequently mentioned.

The Freeway Business Park was a few miles out. He

checked the bus timetables. A bus to St Helens from Halewood, due in the village in five minutes, went within walking distance of the centre.

*

The Freeway Business Park contained about ten units, all steel frame construction with red brick infill and plastic sheet walls and roofs, arranged around a landscaped parking area paved with square brick cobbles. A CCTV camera sat on the first unit covering the entrance. Standard stuff.

He'd have to be careful not to look like a snooper or sneak thief. Best to be brazen about it. He marched along the path that skirted the car park. One unit had been converted to offices. Lots of cars outside. Sign reading *Unit 5 Freeway Investment Services*. He walked up the path and tried the door. Locked.

Back to the bus stop. A bus was waiting but moved off as he broke into a run. He checked the timetable on the side of the post: hourly service. Back to the business park. The first unit was a café: bright strip lights, Formica tables and a smell of frying. The man in front of him in the short queue, most likely a lorry driver, ordered a breadstick breakfast special: bacon, sausages, black pudding and two fried eggs in a large breadstick; lots of sauce; no salad. Martin hadn't had breakfast, so he ordered some toast and a cup of coffee. He took a seat by the window where he could watch the comings and goings.

The toast and coffee arrived, and as he ate he watched

a constant stream of cars, white vans and small wagons. A dark blue Ford Mondeo pulled into a space opposite unit five. A small middle-aged man in a grey suit got out, looked around, then went up to the door of Freeway Investments, unlocked it and went in.

Martin finished the last piece of toast and drained the cup. Things were looking up.

He wandered over to the unit, stepped inside, walked up a flight of stairs and opened the door. A man stood by a filing cabinet with one of the drawers open looking at a file through large, gold-rimmed spectacles with pink lenses. He wore a smart grey suit and open-necked white shirt, not dressed for the beach in Sainsburys this time.

'Well, well,' Martin said. 'Harry Fellows. Long time, no see.'

Fellows squinted at him. 'What are you doing here? You need an appointment. This is private property.'

'Don't you recognise me, Harry? I'd have thought you would, seeing as you were one of the ones who gave me the sack.'

Fellows squinted again. 'Bennett,' he said. 'Martin Bennett.' He laughed, visibly relaxing. 'It must be three years. What've you been up to?'

'Oh, trying to earn a crust. Which can be a little difficult if you've been sacked after people have told a pack of lies about you. Doesn't look good on a job application.'

'It was fair process. The evidence—'

'There was no fucking evidence! Who was behind it? Whitaker? Carter? Your phone number was on his desk.'

'You've obviously been rooting around. I'd leave it if

I were you.'

Martin stepped forward, ready to smack this cunt in the gob. He wasn't a hard man, but he reckoned he could overpower this creep.

'Hey, come on,' Fellows said. 'Let's not get carried away. You're trespassing and now you're threatening me. I think you'd better leave or I'll call the police.' He fixed his gaze on Martin's eyes. 'If I were you ...' His voice became lower, almost inaudible. 'I would look closer to home.'

'Closer to home?' Martin's anger subsided. 'What do you mean?'

'Just think about it.'

'Okay,' Martin said. 'But there's just one thing. What does Benny Carter want to talk to you about?'

Fellows' eyes widened. The name clearly frightened him. 'Benny Carter? Never heard of him. I don't know what you're talking about.' He closed the file, put it on top of the cabinet and shut the drawer. 'I know some important people. People with connections.'

Martin laughed. 'Huh? Gangsters?'

Fellows said nothing. 'And people on the other side,' he said at last. 'You'd be like a nut between a rock and a sledgehammer. It's not worth the risk, mate.' He grinned. 'Now, are you going to leave, or am I going to have to call the police?'

*

The sea was further away than Jimmy thought it would

be. He wore his green Barbour jacket and hiking boots and, with a bird book in his pocket and binoculars round his neck, he strode out like the chartered surveyor with the bird-watching hobby that he was supposed to be. His route led from where he had parked his car in an estate of big Victorian villas, set in huge gardens behind high stone walls, along a wide path to the sea.

Few people were out at this time on a weekday—just the odd person in the distance walking a dog.

He came to a line of sand dunes and took what seemed to be the line of least resistance—a valley between two dunes—but it was still hard going uphill in soft sand. You took a step upwards, and if you weren't careful you slid back to where you'd started from. He reached the crest and paused, breathing hard, a fresh wind off the sea in his face. The drone of an unseen plane somewhere overhead. Now he could see the line of surf in the distance across miles of flat sands under a washed-out sky. The Wirral coast and lines of wind turbines beyond. A solitary jogger to the left, with the cranes of Liverpool docks beyond. Figures everywhere, spread out over the beach. The closest ones looked like the bronze statues they were, but the ones farther out could easily be mistaken for real people standing looking out to sea. One close at hand had been outfitted with a T-shirt by some local wag and one was half buried in the sand.

A big sign warned *Dangerous Coastline – please stay on the path* in red letters on a white background. You had to be careful here. The tide came in so quickly that you could easily be stranded on a strip of sand with the water coming in behind you. Only the week before, there'd been a big rescue involving the lifeboat and helicopters when some kids had been stranded and nearly drowned. Now if you handcuffed someone to a statue, at twilight, say, when there was no one around, it would only take half an hour for the water to come in and drown them. You'd have to check the tides, of course.

He could see a single person way out, moving. He lifted his binoculars and focussed. Not a statue. A small man in a green cap, green Barbour jacket like his own, and green wellies.

'Benny Carter,' he said to himself. 'The little green man. Let's get down to business and sort out this green belt malarkey.'

*

Martin touched the cut and examined his finger. Blood. He'd cut himself shaving several hours ago and it'd still not stopped bleeding. And his legs and back were stiff. It was the pills. He considered the list on the wall.

Leads
Benny Carter
Harry Fellows
Ben Hammond
Gayle Hardin
Julie Bennett
Debbie Bennett
Suspects
Amy Hopkins— a line through it

Lester Adams— a line through it

Mick Malone

Irish gangsters

He'd reached a dead end. He sat slouched in the chair for a few minutes and began to drift off to sleep. An idea came. He sat upright and reached for the telephone directory.

CHAPTER TWENTY-FOUR

The St Helens council housing estate stretched as far as Martin could see. The bus route ran through the middle, but the estate was so large that it was quite a task to walk anywhere. Getting to the schools or the shops would keep you fit. The identical, small, semi-detached houses were constructed in common brick, apart from the ones that'd been rendered or faced with artificial stone. From the incredible variety of roofing materials, windows and fencing, it looked as if nearly all of them had been sold off. Many of the gardens had been converted to hard standings, but the gardens that remained were nearly all neat and well-kept.

Number fifty-two Attlee Crescent—he'd passed Bevan Gardens and Wilson Road—was one of the ones faced with artificial stone. A grey Ford Focus stood on a hard-standing. The bit of garden left was immaculate.

He'd rung ahead, and they were expecting him. Mrs Hardin—small, stern and expressionless—showed him into the front room. Martin perched on the leather sofa, and she went to make tea. A vague smell of boiled cabbage and burnt sausage pervaded the house. The fireplace was made of the same artificial stone as on the front of the house—it'd probably been left over. A leather pouf sat next to the sofa—he'd not seen one of them for years. A big picture over the mantelpiece showed a stag on an outcrop of rock perched over what looked like a Scottish glen.

An electric fire blasted out heat; the artificial coals glowed red. Too hot, he squirmed on the leather. It squeaked. Fragile-looking ornaments, glasses and figurines filled a glass cabinet in one corner. He felt a strange urge to kick the cabinet to see how many objects would break.

Someone coughed in the next room. Whoever it was fought for breath for what seemed like minutes, straining until eventually a conclusion was reached, the throat was cleared and then silence.

Mrs Hardin came in with a tray. 'Don't take any notice of Mr Hardin,' she said. 'He's got emphysema. It won't be long now.'

Her tone surprised Martin. She sounded as if she'd remarked on a hinge creaking or something in the garden sighing in the wind. She sat down and they contemplated each other over mugs of tea. Martin took a sip—too much milk and what tasted like several heaped spoonfuls of sugar.

'I remember you coming round to pick up John to go climbing,' she said. 'I never liked him doing that climbing. Too dangerous. Tennis would've been more to my liking. Everything so clean and white. In those days, anyway. It's all changed now. Do you play tennis, Martin?'

'Not my game, Mrs Hardin. I'm more into climbing

and running. Well, not so much of either now, injuries and all that.'

Tears coursed down her cheeks and into the deep lines by the sides of her mouth. 'Why did they cremate him without informing us? Why would anyone do that?'

'I don't know.' Martin said. Should he tell her about the murder on the escalator? He chickened out. 'I'm sorry. He was a good friend. I just want you to know that.' It was a lie, but what the heck.

She stared at him. The tears stopped but her face remained wet. 'He wasn't our real son, you know; he was adopted.'

Martin raised an eyebrow.

A coughing fit started in the next room, and they sat listening without speaking. A dog barked in the near distance, as if echoing the coughing, which reached a crescendo of wheezing and gasping and then silence. The dog stopped barking too.

'John was a nice kid,' she said. 'Lively. Always in trouble, but never for anything nasty. He didn't have a nasty bone in his body. There was the trouble with the drugs, of course. But taking drugs is a sign of weakness, not nastiness, don't you think? Anyhow, when he started climbing that sorted things out. He was good at something. He blossomed. Got a job at the outdoor centre, and he was on his way. Didn't come home much, but you can't blame him for that. We're not his real parents, like I said. He never knew his mother.' She sniffed and wiped her eyes with a tissue.

'Well, Mrs Hardin,' he said at last. 'I'll have to be going. Could I use your loo?'

'Of course—top of the stairs, straight ahead.'

The tiny bedroom, half of it constricted by a sloping ceiling, had a bed tucked against the outside wall under a window. Martin heard another wheezing fit starting downstairs. He sat on the bed and wondered what it would've been like to sleep in such a tiny room and be brought up by people who weren't your mother and father. He imagined lying awake at night wondering about your real parents.

Some Airfix models hung from the ceiling from threads—a Heinkel bomber with a Spitfire in pursuit. The models had been carefully painted and the gun turrets and propellers rotated easily.

The bookshelf housed climbing books and ones on big game hunting. Martin flicked through one: a bearded hunter posed with dead lions, buffalo, an elephant. Surprising. John had always made himself out to be a bit of a hippy. An old-fashioned Little Imps tin sat in the corner of the shelf. The top took a bit of levering off. The tin was empty, though it still gave off a strong smell of liquorice and menthol.

'Martin?' came a voice from the bottom of the stairs.

He went into the toilet and flushed the cistern. 'Sorry,' he shouted, 'just coming.'

CHAPTER TWENTY-FIVE

'Steady as we go, sunbeam,' a voice breathed in Martin's ear. A strong hand gripped his arm, stopping him from turning the key in the front door lock.

'Just get in the car.'

Martin began to protest, but he was thrust into the back seat of a big grey Merc with darkened windows. A carrier bag was shoved over his head, and the car moved away.

Paralyzed with fear, he put up no resistance. Someone big squashed up against him—big and silent. The journey lasted about twenty minutes and, from the number of stops, presumably at lights, and the noise of traffic, he guessed they were heading into the city centre.

Once the driver said something Martin couldn't catch, but he recognised the high-pitched voice.

'What was that?' Martin said.

'I said that you were in the Old Cop Shop the other night. Were you following me?'

'Not at all.' Martin tried to sound innocent.

'Well, just remember this; round here nosey fuckers tend to end up like grasses.' A long pause. 'Nailed up and bleeding.'

They drove into an echoing space. An underground car park? The big bloke manoeuvred him into what must be a lift. The ascent seemed to take a long time. A high building? He was led through what must be several doors, and then his hood was removed. He was in a penthouse suite overlooking the Mersey with the Wirral skyline on the opposite bank and the slowly moving lights of the wheel. A high-backed chair by the window swivelled and a man stood up: average build, high forehead, glasses; black, thinning hair swept back; pullover, shirt and trousers; looked like an accountant rather than a gangster.

'Ah, Mr Bennett, we've been expecting you!' The man burst out laughing. 'Sorry, I'm a bit of a James Bond movie fan. Quite a view, isn't it?'

Martin tried to memorise the details of the view so he could identify the penthouse's location later. The room was bigger than all the rooms of his house added together.

'Here, have a seat,' the man said, as if it were a business meeting. 'Coffee?' He motioned with his head.

'No, thanks.' Martin sat on an easy chair. Something small and hard pressed into his bum.

The man shrugged and poured himself a cup. 'I'm Jimmy Hughes,' he said. 'Sorry about all the theatrics, but in the business I'm in I can't take chances.' He looked at Martin as if about to ask a question. 'Come and have a look this.'

He motioned with his arm, walked to the doorway to another room and went in. Martin stood and checked what he'd been sitting on. A small automatic, like a toy gun, lay there, but on careful observation he realised it was real. He slipped it into his pocket. At least now he had some protection.

'Come on,' Hughes said from the doorway. 'I want you to see this.'

Martin walked to the door and looked in. He didn't think Hughes had seen him pocket the gun. The room was smaller than the first one and more rectangular, maybe ten metres by five. A model of Liverpool's water-front—Liver Buildings, Albert Dock, Pierhead—almost took up the whole of the floor. Except that it was different—older, no wheel.

'It's set in 1956 when the overhead railway closed down.' Hughes picked up a gadget—the sort of thing a kid would use to control a model car—and pushed a button. A train hummed along an elevated railway. 'Seaforth to the Dingle. Fantastic, isn't it? We own all sorts of property round here, but when I saw this place I had to have it for myself. The feller who owned it spent most of his life building it and collecting these.' Hughes waved an arm at a wall covered with shelves packed with models of ships. 'Died suddenly of a heart attack. Spent all his money on it, so I got everything in a job lot.'

Martin walked over and examined the largest model.

'So you own property round here?' he said.

'Sure do. Or rather Mersey Estates, my company, does. All over the city. And its outskirts. Trouble is, we can't develop on most of it.'

'Why's that, then?'

'It's green belt. Only fit for growing carrots. Don't pretend, Mr Bennett.' Hughes' voice was harder now. 'You work for Lester Adams at Development Solutions. You know all about green belts.'

Silence for a few moments.

'Nice model,' Martin said.

'That's the Titanic. The offices of the shipping line were in this building.' The model train reached the Dingle end of the line and rolled into a large tunnel. 'They cut through miles of sandstone at that end. They go right to the docks. The model's perfect, everything to scale.' The train emerged from the tunnel. Hughes pressed a button and it gave a little toot.

'Can you get through the tunnels now?' Martin said. 'Aren't they flooded? I heard a kid drowned down there.'

'Not completely. There's sumps that are God knows how deep, but according to local folklore you can get through. You just need a pair of wellies and a pole, and not panic. There's a ledge about a foot wide on the left looking down to the river. Keeps the scallies out. Come on,' he said, leading Martin back into the other room. He sat down and faced Martin. 'Go on, have a seat.'

Martin sat.

'Okay, to business,' Hughes continued. 'We have a mutual friend. Had a mutual friend. Mr Hardin.'

Martin snorted. 'He was hardly a friend. I hadn't seen him for years before he turned up a few days ago.'

'Aha. Well, Mr Hardin happened to owe us some money. A lot of money. Maybe you know something about it?'

'Like I said. I knew him years ago. I only talked with him briefly five days ago.'

'Right. You know what kind of business we're in?'

'No.'

'We merchandise certain goods. These goods get delivered to us wholesale. We pay and then distribute them retail. Got it?'

He must be talking about drugs. A cold sensation of fear crept up Martin's back.

'Mr Hardin was handling a wholesale transaction for us,' Hughes continued, 'and claimed to have been robbed of the cash and merchandise. A claim we have reason to doubt. His death was extremely inconvenient for us. We would like to locate the stolen items.'

'I honestly know nothing about any of this.'

Hughes narrowed his eyes at Martin. His hair could've been brushed on with black gloss paint. He seemed amiable enough, but there was an underlying certainty about the way he carried himself.

'Maybe you don't,' Hughes said. 'We're not mad-dog gangsters, you know. We can be reasonable about things. For myself, I'd prefer to get out of anything messy and concentrate on Mersey Estates and sort out a few problems there like the green belt land I mentioned before. This present dilemma with Mr Hardin and yourself is the last loose end before I realise that ambition. I want you to go away and think about this.' He paused. 'I understand that you have been making enquiries about Mr Hardin.'

Martin thought for a long time. Maybe this man, who looked more like an accountant than a thug, was telling the truth. If so, he wouldn't have wanted John dead. Might as well go for it. 'I think he was murdered,' he said.

'But he had a heart attack.'

'I saw someone inject him with something on the hospital escalator.'

'Well, it wasn't us. Why would we kill him when he owed us big time? We'd have got the truth out of him first, wouldn't we? Same goes for our suppliers. They're not happy. Blaming us. We want that money. Anyone who tried to stop us achieving that goal would incur a risk. A very great risk.'

The door opened and Malone and Gobby came in. Big and even bigger. They put the hood over his head again and ushered him down to the car.

'I know where your daughter lives, Bennett,' the driver said in that high-pitched squeaky voice. 'I know where she works. I know when she has her lunch, and I know where she goes for a shit.'

'How do you know that?' Martin managed to stutter.

'How? Let's just say that I've got some good friends high up in this city. They've checked up on you. You know something about Hardin and his clever capers. Just remember I'm not like that soft lad back up in his penthouse playing with his train set. Anyone crosses me and they end up on the cross. And if it's a tart I fuck 'em first.'

Martin was doubly shocked—by the man's violent threat to his daughter and also by the realisation that if this thug was open about having good friends high up in the city, Martin couldn't go to the police. Robinson would be no use. He would just get steam-rolled over.

At least he had some protection now. They'd searched him on the way in but hadn't bothered on the way out. Why would they? He fingered the gun in his pocket. Small, like a toy, but at close quarters deadly enough.

CHAPTER TWENTY-SIX

Jane poured herself a large glass of Merlot, put on a Leonard Cohen CD and settled back on the sofa. Bruce lay at her feet, stitched up and feeling sorry for himself, with a plastic cone on his head to stop him worrying the wound. The alcohol with the tablets would make her feel strange, but she didn't care. She now had three problems to sort out. Leonard was singing, 'I fought against the bottle, but I had to do it drunk …' She laughed out loud. How appropriate. She took a slug of wine.

First problem: Cath Benson had stopped her in the corridor, checked that no one was listening in and asked for an update on 'our little investigation'.

All Jane could say was that she was working on it and would have something in a couple of days. Cath had given her a long look, then said, 'Two days? I'll hold you to that.' The trouble was that, despite having access to Whitaker's files and email correspondence, the cunning asshole had obviously covered his tracks and eliminated anything incriminating.

The second problem was that Whitaker himself was all over her like a rash, leaving messages on her mobile every five minutes. For some reason, he was fixated on this green belt/housing strategy thing. Presumably it was political. Everyone knew he was talking to UKIP, even though he officially denied it. Maybe he was slated for one of their shadow cabinet posts. Shadow cabinet? That was a laugh.

The final problem was Ann Smith. Things weren't getting any better. When Jane had asked her how she was getting on with the new filing system, Ann had ignored her and walked off. The last thing Jane needed was a problem member of staff. Ann was supposed to provide administrative support, but apart from the most mundane tasks it was easier and more straightforward for Jane to do them herself.

From long experience, Jane now insisted on having a proper filing system, paper and virtual. Each file had to have a master sheet at the front with the key actions set out together with the date and tick boxes for key actions—each of which had to be colour coded. At first glance it looked a bit anally retentive, but staff came and went, and you usually picked up an old file when there was an emergency, and no one knew enough about the issue to answer questions.

Once she'd been caught out by having to cover for one of her managers who'd gone off sick just before a European Commission audit. She'd been intensely embarrassed when the Swedish auditor had given her an hour to find a missing file or he would report back to the commission. In the end, they had to cobble together a file from the e-mail history and officers' notes.

If Jane had been in complete charge she would've given Ann a formal warning, but she could hardly go to

Whitaker and Cath Benson with such a course of action at the moment.

She took a sip of wine and leaned back on the sofa. Leonard was singing, 'Did I ever love you? Did I ever need you? Did I ever fight you? Did I ever want to?' A tear eased into her eye and she wiped it away in anger.

Bruce sat up and listened. He ambled over to the conservatory doors and let out a low whine.

'Want a piddle, do you, mate?' she said, ruffling his head. She let him out and waited at the door. A full moon with a bright Jupiter close by brilliantly lit the clear night sky.

Bruce barked, the sound, deep and gruff, not like a golden retriever, more like a mastiff.

'At least you bark a good fight,' she said,

He stood by the back fence now, barking at something on the other side. She'd seen foxes several times on the nearby roads and in the park. Once she'd seen one ambling down the main village street as if it owned the place. She went down to see what was going on, but when she got to the fence, something hit her on the head, something not heavy and dampish. Bruce ambled out and tried to grab whatever it was, but the cone, which scraped on the ground, stopped him. She grabbed him by the collar and only just managed to hold him back. She followed the direction of his straining nose and found it. A piece of meat?

She dragged Bruce inside, slammed the door shut, then ran round the house making sure all the doors and windows were locked. She walked back to the kitchen and examined the piece of meat lying on the floor where she'd thrown it. Something had to be done. This was a direct physical threat, worse than Ann Smith, Cath Benson and James Whitaker put together. She had to fight back somehow. It would be risky, and she couldn't go to the police with this business with Whitaker hanging over her head. Was she up to it?

She could hardly use force; Steven was much stronger than her. And even when fully fit, Bruce was no use as a guard dog. She could buy a pepper spray or a baseball bat, but what if she only hurt and enraged him? That would make things worse. He might kill her. But if a large, dangerous animal hunted you, you wouldn't have to physically fight it. You could lay a trap and use the creature's greater physical strength against itself. And it absolved you of any blame or moral qualms. It would be the creature's own fault. So long as there were no witnesses.

*

Parking spaces were rare in Gambier Terrace and, to Martin's anger, he had to pay at a machine.

It seemed so obvious now. The tunnel in the cathedral quarry was right below Gambier Terrace. John would've remembered it from when they used to sit in the entrance to the tunnel and smoke dope all those years ago. The obvious place to hide. The obvious place to hide stuff.

Climbing into the cave in wellies in the gathering darkness was more difficult than he'd thought it would be. He had to throw up the wooden pole and hold the flashlight between his teeth like a pirate. You couldn't carry that lot onto a bus or into a taxi without someone noticing and remembering, so he'd had to use the car.

He'd googled the history of the Liverpool tunnels. In the nineteenth century an eccentric philanthropist, Joseph Williamson, had employed hundreds of men to dig a huge and elaborate system of tunnels, chambers and passageways under Liverpool. Later in the century a railway tunnel had been built from the docks to Edge Hill, intended to provide a link to Manchester. Ventilation shafts remained as local landmarks. The line had closed in the 1970s, but as far as he could make out the tunnel was still there.

Sand and rock lay underfoot and cool air flowed into his face. Negotiating the tunnel was much easier with the flashlight; now he could see the details of the tunnel walls, the diagonal chip-marks from the stonemasons' tools and the horizontal bands of lighter-coloured, yellowish rock in the red sandstone.

He came to the water and tested it with the pole. It went in and kept going. He had to haul it back to avoid losing it. He tested the area by the tunnel wall on the left. Only about six inches deep and twelve wide. He walked through the water slowly, testing with the pole as he went. After twenty metres he reached dry land.

He followed the tunnel for a short way, then came to a junction where a modern tunnel, circular and made of concrete, led off. He tried to orient himself. This tunnel seemed to be heading due east parallel to the river and was lower, only just high enough to walk along. It had a layer of sand on the floor which muffled his footsteps and felt a lot more claustrophobic than the old one. He followed it for a long way until he came to steps leading up to a steel door. It creaked open.

The door sat in a low, red-brick structure in an open area off wasteland filled with half-grown trees surrounded by a steel palisade fence. A track led to the fence, which looked intact, but when he examined it, he found that one of the holding bolts had been cut through, then replaced so it would look intact to a casual observer. He climbed through into a deserted street: Belvedere Drive, only a few yards from Gayle's house. He could drop in for a chat. He considered this. No.

He went all the way back to the tunnel junction, walking as fast as he could and trying not to panic as the feeling of claustrophobia intensified, then he headed on towards the river. He was building up a sweat; these tunnels stretched for much further than he'd imagined. A large cave was set at right angles to the tunnel. He walked on with the tunnel curving towards the river. After a hundred yards or so, the tunnel ended at a set of steps carved into the rock. They led up to another steel door. When he opened it, bright lights overhead dazzled him. When his eyes adjusted to the light, he saw the top of the Liverpool Wheel not far away over the tops of buildings, another patch of wasteland, strewn with bricks and rubbish, and another steel fence—and, yes, the same trick with the cut bolt.

Right, he knew where he was and how the tunnel system worked. He walked back to the cave and found it opened out into a large space. In the centre stood a giant stone sarcophagus, complete with a heavy lid like in a horror movie. He shone the light around the cave and noticed an alcove set into a side wall. He walked over and shone the light in. Two dark blue canvas holdalls sat there, the sort you'd take on an overnight trip. They looked new. You couldn't see them from the tunnel itself. He opened the zip on one. Inside sat bundles of banknotes wrapped in plastic. The second held fat plastic bags of something white like sugar.

He zipped the bags back up, thought for a moment, then carried them over to the sarcophagus. He tried to move the lid, but it refused to budge. He felt a surge of panic. Suppose the tomb wasn't empty? There might be a skeleton inside. Or worse. Like in the vampire films.

He took several deep breaths and managed to control his breathing. Not a good place for a stroke, deep underground. Again he tried to shift the lid, using all his strength. This time it slid slowly across until he'd made a two foot gap. He shone the torch in. Empty. He slid the bags in and dragged the lid back to where it'd been. Now he noticed that someone had painted a symbol on top of the lid. The red paint didn't stand out against the blackened sandstone. It looked like some kind of devil worship symbol. They'd come here for their rituals.

Something scrabbled in the corner of the cave. A rat? He ran, the flashlight playing crazily on the tunnel walls as he stumbled back towards the entrance. In his panic, he slipped while traversing the pool and only just saved himself by scrabbling at the brick wall.

*

A breeze gusted down the street, and it'd just started to drizzle, so someone with his coat hood pulled over his head most likely wouldn't draw attention. To add to the disguise, Whitaker wore an old pair of reading glasses. He wouldn't want to be recognised by some passing balloonhead on this little caper, that was for sure.

He'd been watching the entrance to the second annexe from a shop doorway opposite for some time. Only a couple of lights remained on in the building now. The porter's office was dark. If the worst came to the worst he could always blag his way out of it. Retrieving an important document. Something like that. But he'd prefer not to have to.

He strode onto the street and crossed over, the torch heavy in his pocket. He tried the door—unlocked—then walked slowly through the foyer, got out the fob card and slid it over the security plate by the side of the door. He pushed the door and it opened. At least something worked. Though if you were going to spend anything on a building like this, it would be on security.

The last time he'd been in the building they'd shown the developers around. A run-down pigsty. Embarrassing. Nothing had been spent on maintenance for years. But then the architect's report had noted that, despite the decor being totally run-down, the steel frame was sound. The plan was to convert it to one bedroom flats for yuppies or students, and you had to take it down to its shell anyway. So they hoped to get a good price for it.

He made a mental note to chivvy along the sorting out of the staffing issues. The building was used as a temporary home for the sick, lame and lazy left over from downsizing in departments all over the city. His own admin support team were based there for the moment. He'd have to get Jane to sort out a more permanent home. Though it might not be so permanent for Jane. Sometimes you made a mistake in hiring and firing, but the thing was to sort it out with whatever measure of ruthlessness was required and move on.

He avoided turning any lights on, moving up the stairs guided by the streetlights outside. Third floor: old environmental health department.

A noise. He stopped at the top of the stairs and listened. Nothing. This was it. He opened the door, went in and closed it. The musty smell of old documents tickled his nose. He switched on the torch and looked around, being careful not to shine it near the windows. You couldn't see them for racks of big cardboard boxes that reached to the ceiling but better to be safe than sorry. At the end of the room stood a door with a sign: *Mr S. Andrews Chief Environmental Health Officer.* He searched along the racks, checking off the labels against the schedule he'd printed off.

Eventually he found the box containing the project files. He lifted it down. The bastard was heavy and covered in dust. He checked through the files, found what he was looking for, then put the box back and went with the file towards the door. Something stirred somewhere. He stopped and listened. All quiet. He exited the back way, past the bins, but the beam of a torch flashed across the wall in front of him. A security guard. It wouldn't do for the mayor of Liverpool to be caught red-handed stealing a file. Best get rid of it. He lifted the lid on the nearest bin and thrust in the file.

'Best place for you, my lad.'

*

Martin had finalised the four tracks for his playlist: *We Can Talk About It Now—The Band; Does This Bus Stop At 21st Street—Bruce Springsteen; Boogie Woogy Waltz—Weather Report; Alone Again Or—Love.* All unashamed upbeat hippie stuff, the sort of music that would get people of a certain age dreaming of golden days smoking dope and tripping on acid. But the Weather Report track was long; maybe it should go first with Brucy second and Love third. Finish with The Band. He couldn't decide.

He leaned back in his seat. All quiet. Too early for rowdies from the pubs. And Lemmy and Motorhead must have done the trick with the neighbours. He considered the list on the wall. The trail had gone cold with Fellows and Benny Carter, and the visit to John's childhood home had been unproductive. Robinson's tip had led him to Mick Malone and Jimmy Hughes. The obvious question was: why would they kill John when they wanted the money and the drugs? Martin now knew about them, and such knowledge was dangerous. Should he tell Robinson? No point if his superiors were in with Malone, who was obviously a psycho, capable of any violence to get what he

232

wanted. But if he was pally with people at the top, how could Martin go to the police for protection? And if his daughter was now under threat what could he do about it? He had a gun, but if he used it on Malone they would fit him up and throw the book at him.

Maybe a convenient accident would remove the threat with no risk to himself. Shooting someone was clear murder, even if the victim was a dangerous psycho like Malone. But if he suffered an accident while chasing you to murder you and your precious daughter, that was his own fault and good riddance. He could go out and get a takeaway and some bottles. No, there was one option left on the list. He reached for the phone but it rang before he could dial.

*

Jimmy Hughes ran the train one more time, watching with pride as it sped along the overhead railway then disappeared into the tunnel. He waited until it appeared at the other end by the Liver Buildings then shut down the power. He walked over to the window and took in the view for a moment. The slowly moving lights on the wheel shone bright in the darkness. Yes, the job had to be done. Whatever the risk. He turned. Now where had he put that bloody gun?

CHAPTER TWENTY-SEVEN

As soon as Martin moved, a hangover headache struck him. Gayle lay beside him, her skin remarkably smooth and tanned. Did she go to a salon? He resisted a strong urge to stroke her short, blonde hair. Feeling stiff all over, he moved a foot, but a spasm of cramp locked it into place. He suppressed a cry of pain, reached down and bent the foot back until the spasm passed. The pills!

Something small and hard stuck to his bum. A piece of grit? He slipped out of bed and pulled off a little, black rectangular sweet. He sniffed it. Liquorice and menthol. He put it in a wastepaper basket and went down to make coffee. Strong coffee.

He stood by the kettle, waiting for it to boil. Nice kitchen. He examined one of the cupboard doors—real oak—then walked into the lounge. It was furnished from antique shops, very tasteful and expensive, the most striking object a large, patterned Persian carpet that covered an entire wall.

He remembered why he'd come in the first place: the threatening phone call; someone prowling around the house. Best give the place a look over and check security. The layout was much like his own house: two up, two down, terraced, front door, back door, both with mortice locks, modern plastic windows—the top opening made it difficult to climb in. He walked quietly up the stairs with the mugs of coffee. Three rooms on the first floor. Main bedroom—with Gayle still asleep. Bathroom. Back bedroom. The door to this was locked. Why lock the door to a spare bedroom?

When he walked in with the coffee she was awake, staring at him with the duvet held over her mouth. He put her mug on the table by her side of the bed, then went back to his side with his own mug.

'At least you're not fat,' she said, cuddling up to him. 'Well, not very fat.'

'Thank you. You're not too bad yourself.'

'Hah. Well, we got that out of the way without any unpleasantness.' She sat up, picked up the mug and took a swallow of coffee. His eyes were drawn to her breasts, and he had to look away. 'You were sweet last night,' she said. 'God, I was pissed.'

He leaned over and stroked her hand. 'You were nice, too, Gayle. I'm afraid I'm a bit out of practice with this kind of thing.'

'Tell me about it. '

'Come on, where did you learn all that kind of stuff?'

'I'm easily bored.' She grinned at him. 'Would you like breakfast?'

'I feel like being sick at the thought of breakfast.'

'Come on. You'll feel better. We can go for a walk in the park. Fresh air. Nothing like it.'

She joined him in the lounge wearing jeans and a T-shirt.

'Let's just go over this phone call,' Martin said. 'What did this character say?'

'Character? Knobhead, you mean.' She sat down and closed her eyes. 'I can't remember. It was a shock. Something along the lines of me being a nuisance, and if I didn't behave myself he'd come down to where I live, batter the door down, slap my legs, then rape me good and hard. I particularly remember the 'good and hard' bit.'

'Charming.'

'He also said that my house, number five, didn't have many neighbours to hear what was going on so he could take his time.'

'Just to let you know that he knows exactly which house is yours.'

'Right.'

'And this was last night?'

'Yep. About eight o'clock. That's when I rang you.' She opened her eyes and smiled at him. 'I had no one else to turn to.' A pause. 'Do you think it's connected to John? How's the investigation going?'

'Not so well. Red herrings and dead ends.'

'You work with our dear mayor, don't you?' she said. 'Mr James fuckface Whitaker.'

'Kind of. We do consultancy jobs for him and the council.'

'What, like demolishing these houses?' She motioned with her hand.

'We don't actually deal directly with that, but yes, we have provided advice. I don't agree with the official policy, personally.'

'I'm glad to hear it. You're not just saying that?'

'Honest.' He laughed.

'What would you say if I told you that Whitaker is corrupt? I've been doing a bit of research into his background. Remember his campaign opposing organised crime in the city? He was beaten up, wasn't he? Unless it was staged. It was all over the news. That's what clinched the vote. But Mr Whitaker isn't as clean as he makes out. There's a network of organised crime in this city used to launder money. Drugs money. Have you heard of Mersey Estates?'

'Yeah, it's one of the biggest estate agencies in the area.'

'Well, it was set up to buy property using profits from a security company and a construction company. Dirty money was used to pay cash-in-hand workers. And this organisation called the Merseyside Regeneration Agency used the profits from the property company to match European grants and build all sorts of things. Like call centres. And guess who the head of this agency was? Mr James buggerlugs Whitaker. It goes from the bottom right to the top. Have you ever heard of Chuckie Chipchase?'

'Who hasn't? They've written books and made TV programmes about him. Wasn't one of his henchmen murdered by a Mexican cartel and his face stitched onto a football?'

'Wacker Hughes.'

'Right. But Chuckie's banged up for life.'

'No, sir. He'll be out soon, and he'll be expecting his money to be there. But I'm going to blow the gaffe on Mr

James wanker Whitaker. Do you know that's what his staff used to call him?'

'I'd be careful, Gayle. Don't get involved in that kind of thing. It's too risky.'

'I've got nothing to lose, have I?' She started crying.

'Look,' he said. 'I'll do my best.'

*

A gust of wind met them as they left the house. Gayle, still only wearing jeans and a T-shirt, turned away, shivering.

'It's a bit parky!' she cried. 'Wait here and I'll get a coat. And I have to go to the loo.'

Martin leaned against the wall. Gayle's house was one of the few still occupied in the street. Most were boarded up. Where the bricks had been painted over, the paint had come off in large sheets. Weeds grew from gutters and cracks in the pavement. In places, small trees had sprouted up. He got out his phone and read a text from Lester: *Climbing this afternoon? How about Pex. Pick you up at three?*

Martin thought. The wind wasn't too bad, and it would probably clear up later. And he didn't feel so stiff now. Three days had passed since the visit to the climbing wall—before the investigation had started—and he could do with the exercise.

OK, he texted. *Ready to be burned off again?*

A white car cruised down the street. It crunched over a brick, stopped opposite Martin and the window slid down. A bearded, middle-aged face appeared—a little anxious.

'Lady Strictly in for business?'

'What?' Martin said.

The man gazed at him for a moment, then looked nervously up and down the street. The window slid up and the car drove off.

*

A reggae band was playing at the park, the heavy bass notes of *Concrete Jungle* reverberating in the air.

They walked towards the sound.

'It's the festival,' Gayle said. She looked great in jeans, high-heeled, black-leather boots and a sweater under her parka. The band played on a huge stage at one end of a field with various food vans and bouncy castles arranged around the edge. It was early—maybe fifty people sat in scattered groups on the field or strolled past the vans. Kids were screaming and enjoying themselves on the castle. Later on, in the evening, the field would be packed.

She took his hand as they walked. 'So what are we going to do to stop the mayor demolishing our nice houses?' she asked.

'It's a difficult one for me, Gayle. My firm's involved.'

'So you've taken the thirty pieces of silver?' She squeezed his hand and put her arm around his waist. 'Only joking!' she laughed.

'I'll see what I can do,' he said. 'But hang fire on that exposure of the underworld stuff. Promise?'

She nodded.

He wondered if this was a good time to raise the subject of her number being on John's iPad when she supposedly hated the sight of him. Maybe not.

'Fancy a West Indian goat curry?' she said.

'Jokin', aren' ya!'

CHAPTER TWENTY-EIGHT

Steven put his bag in the back of the van and sat for a moment, thinking. He'd decided not to go for gold with Sally. Despite all his compliments, she was a bit past it. He'd gone for a meal and a couple of pints in the hotel bar/restaurant by himself and then settled for an early night.

The trouble with bedding a strange woman on a one-night stand was that, in his experience, it was rarely satisfactory. Better a good fantasy in peace.

He'd lain in bed in the dark and enjoyed his favourite scenario. Jane would be on her knees before him, begging for forgiveness and to be taken back. He stiffened with excitement in the front seat of the van, put his right hand in his trouser pocket and closed his eyes.

She'd pull his trousers down and begin to serve him. He'd let her go on—her sobs and slurps muffled. At the point of orgasm he'd grip her head in both hands, lean down and whisper in an ear: 'It would be nice to take you back, baby, but it's too late now. The horse has bolted, the bird has flown, to you, little lady, the door is shown.'

One twist and her neck would snap. The fantasy never failed to deliver. But not now. He opened his eyes and pulled his hand out of his pants.

It might've worked with Sally. He felt a twinge of regret. But every cloud has its silver lining. If you don't have rain, you won't have the rainbow. She'd given him the lowdown on Sheila and plenty of ammo for his report. Like her regular visits to the golf course and giving the ball loads of wellie. Couldn't walk or tie her own shoelaces, indeed. A video of her demonstrating the golf swing would be great evidence, but it wasn't needed. The stuff in the gym was perfect. In any case, he had e-mailed it over to the ranch from his laptop while enjoying a full English in the hotel restaurant.

His mobile rang.

'It's Bobby here. Thanks for the tape.' Pause. 'The only problem is that something's gone wrong; I can't make out a thing. The camera must have got knocked or something …'

Pause. *Shit.*

'Bobby, you're joking,' Steven moaned. 'Tell me you're joking!'

CHAPTER TWENTY-NINE

James Whitaker had seen the view from Helsby Hill over Merseyside many times, but it still impressed him. On this spring day the sun was hidden but the sky was still bright. Immediately below ran the motorway, six lines of traffic. Beyond, chemical works with columns of fire and smoke, the bright sheet of the Mersey with Hale lighthouse, the two cathedrals, Post Office tower, the Pier Head, the wheel, tower blocks, in the distance the sea and to the left, the undulating line of the Welsh Hills.

The path rose to the edge of a sandstone cliff ahead. He had to crouch down and steady himself with his hands. The rock strata sloped to the edge, and it was obvious that if you weren't careful you could slide over it. Luckily, he wore hiking boots with a vibram sole that gripped the rock well. He peered over the edge. He stood well above the tops of mature trees, maybe eighty feet above the bottom.

He clambered into a grassy bay just below the crest, hidden from the world above and with the expanse of space below. Joseph Stalin had the right idea: 'No man, no problem.' Best not be sexist. 'No person, no problem.' He chuckled out loud. He'd have to be totally PC if he was to get where he wanted to be.

'Today Merseyside, tomorrow the world!'

He turned and saw Benny Carter. He must have come up another way. In his green Barbour jacket, cap and binoculars, he actually looked like a bird-watcher. Except for the shiny, black leather shoes. Balloonhead.

'How does it feel to be master of the universe?' Carter said as he walked down the grass slope. 'Well, master of Merseyside.'

'You're about as funny as piles, Carter,' Whitaker said. 'Actually, it feels great, but it won't last. The other party have pledged to repeal the legislation if they get in, and judging from the latest polls that's quite a likely outcome. What's all the rush? And watch that step. Though I suppose you could always make a trip claim against the National Trust. Do you still have that sign up in front of your offices: *Crash? Whiplash!*'

'Ho, ho, ho,' Carter said as he sat on a boulder a few feet away. 'What's this about you talking to UKIP concerning one of their safe seats?'

'As Winston Churchill said—I'd talk to the devil himself if I thought it would help achieve victory.' Whitaker thought for a moment. 'I hear you've got your own problems.'

'You could say that.'

'Bad publicity? Hey, you could do a telly advert like that crooked lawyer in *Breaking Bad*: In shtuck agen? Better call Ben!'

Carter thought for a moment. 'Defence a non-starter?' he said. 'Better call Carter!'

'Something like that. Needs to be a bit snappier,

though. Are you still acting for that footballer, Tony Gazelle? The feller with the pink Mohican? The referee should book him for having an offensive hairstyle.'

'Sure am. The lad's a gold mine. He got stopped for speeding in his hundred-thousand-pound Porsche the other day and had never heard of a driving licence or car insurance. Not much call for them on the estate where he was brought up.'

'And Chuckie?'

Carter looked round. 'So, so. It's the feller who's in charge now who's causing the problems. Wacker's nephew, Jimmy. Seems like Mersey Estates is about to go pop.'

'That's nothing to do with me these days.'

'I know, but this Jimmy Hughes is desperate. He's lost it. Threatening to blow the whistle if it all goes down. He looks like a wimp compared to your standard thug, but he's more dangerous. He's not a loose cannon, he's a fucking twenty-ton bulldozer that's out of control. He'd take us both down with him.'

Whitaker thought. How far was he prepared to go?

'The last thing I need at the moment,' he said, 'is any hint of a connection to organised crime. What do they call it? The end of a political career?' He thought again for a moment. 'Couldn't we get him dealt with? Put him to bed with the fishes?'

Carter laughed. 'Oh yeah!' he said. 'I assume you are joking! In the cast list I'm the corrupt solicitor, you're the corrupt politician and Jimmy's the gangster. No, we'll have to go along with him.'

'What's his problem?'

Carter pulled a face. 'It's this housing shite. He needs planning permission for all this land Mersey Estates owns in the green belt. I thought you were going to get the policy changed.'

'It's not that simple. It's one of the things that need the permission of the people in Whitehall. If I can make a good enough case they might approve it. Everyone wants to increase the rate of housebuilding these days. There's pundits and professors and all kinds of experts saying we should relax the green belt controls. I've got the team working on it.'

'Well, this team of yours will have to be quick. I don't think I can keep Jimmy Hughes on the leash for long.'

Was it time for a call to Chewie? Remind him of his obligations? A call was always risky, but he could make it as brief as possible on a spare moby then dump.

A sudden cacophony of deep, guttural caws and high-pitched screams came from off to one side. Three big, black birds and two smaller ones—both coloured grey and brown—swirled in the sky, attacking each other. One of the big black ones intertwined its talons with one of the smaller ones, and they swung downwards, parting just before they reached the ground. Whitaker tried to remember from his bird watching days with Chuckie. Ravens. The big black birds were ravens.

'Ravens and peregrines,' Carter said. 'They don't get on. Each will steal the others' chicks.'

'Ravens have got a bad reputation, haven't they?'

'They're supposed to be unlucky. Carrion birds, like vultures. They used to hang around the scaffold in the olden days to eat the bodies of hanged men.'

'Aren't there some at the Tower of London?'

'Yup. There's a tale that if they ever leave, the kingdom of England will fall. In Charles the Second's time the astronomers used to watch the stars from the Tower. They got fed up with the noise of the birds and were about to get rid of them, but the king put a stop to it and moved the astronomers to Greenwich instead. And in the Second World War they were frightened off by the bombing or died of shock. They were put back at the end of the war, but it was too late. Britain went into decline and lost its empire.'

They stared out over the estuary.

'That's quite a view,' Whitaker said. 'The chemical works and the motorway spoil it, though.'

'And talking of empires,' Carter continued, on a roll now, 'there was a signal station here in Roman times on the edge of their empire. They had a dig in the Twenties and found a bronze statue of an emperor. It's in a museum in Chester. The station replaced an Iron Age fort. You can find the outline of it if you search around. Imagine the view then, sitting up here watching out for invading barbarian hordes.'

'The woolly backs from Lancashire, you mean?'

They enjoyed the view over the Mersey for a few minutes in silence.

'And don't forget, James,' Carter said, 'that, if the worst comes to the worst, I've got enough evidence on you to take you down with me. I'll go queen's evidence.'

Whitaker stared at Carter's feet and wondered how

far he was prepared to go to reach the top, to get rid of obstacles standing in the way of his ambitions despite the obvious risks. If it wasn't for the risks, this kind of thing could be exciting, addictive even. But then, he realised, it was exciting because of the risks.

One of the lawyer's shoes was turned slightly to one side, revealing a bright yellow leather sole. Very slippery.

*

Martin considered the list. He'd followed every lead, and they'd all hit a dead end. What to do about the stash and the cash? It was a dangerous millstone around his neck. And its existence endangered not only himself but also his daughter. Maybe take some of the money? No, it was dirty money. Traceable. And he couldn't even hand it back. He was a witness who knew too much.

But one lead might not have hit a dead end. He googled *Lady Strictly* and came up with a website offering high-class VIP companions for gentlemen and guilty boys who needed to be punished. He skimmed through the photo gallery. The lady hardly looked like Gayle under the thick makeup and with the bizarre uniforms and punishment tools—whips and the like—but it was clearly her. He tapped the Etiquette button. Gentlemen were expected to be polite, respectful, dress nicely, wash their hands and show their ID on arrival. So that was it. End of the lead. Dead end.

He switched off the computer, leaned back in the chair and closed his eyes. After a few moments he opened his eyes and sat up. He had to accept defeat. The investigation was at an end. Might as well relax. He could slaughter a fry-up in the cafe.

No. Time for some exercise.

CHAPTER THIRTY

Lester grunted as the off-roader hit a bump and took to the air. Clearly an off-roader in name only.

'Are you sure this is the way to Pex Hill?' Martin said.

'Nearly lost my toupee and my false teeth there,' Lester said. 'Look for somewhere to turn round.'

Coming through Rainhill, Lester must have taken a wrong turn, and they'd ended up driving down what seemed like a glorified farm track.

They bumped along for several hundred yards with fences and hedges tight up to the track on either side, then came round a corner and met a red and white wagon going fast. Luckily, they were next to an area of grass, and Lester managed to swing their car off the track. The wagon roared by, leaving a cloud of dust. They caught a glimpse of the driver's stony face staring straight ahead.

'What about that?' Lester shouted. 'What a fucking idiot!'

They continued on for a few hundred yards.

'There's the motorway.' Martin pointed at the top of a moving lorry just visible over a hedge. 'And that looks like the Freeway Centre.'

They bumped over a rise and entered a wood.

'Here, you can turn here,' Martin said as they entered

an open area in the wood. 'Watch out for mud.'

The car reversed back and suddenly sank down about six inches. The engine stalled.

'Oh shit!' Lester said. They sat for a few moments. 'We'll have to find some logs or something to put under the wheels.'

Martin got out and looked around. Nothing. He walked a few yards into the trees and saw unpainted, rusty-steel fencing and, beyond, a large shed constructed from plastic sheets that had yellowed with age, with a sign—*Sizzling Sausages*—on its side. A photograph of a panful of frying sausages sat underneath the title with the caption *Locally Produced Quality*. Sheep baa-ed, and an awful smell filled the air. Like when you approached a dead sheep in the hills; you smelt it before you saw it. He walked further. A porta cabin with several cars parked next to it—most likely the site office—came into view.

Someone stepped from behind a tree. An old man in scruffy clothes—and with a leather cap rammed on top of a Willie-Nelson-style, long, grey ponytail which hung down to his waist. He carried a shotgun in the crook of an arm. Martin ran back to the car and jumped in.

'It's him!' he said.

'Who?'

'The farmer with the shotgun and an anger management problem.'

'Oh fuck.'

Lester hammered the gear lever in, and slowly coaxed the car forwards. It suddenly shot out of the mud and they bounced back the way they'd come. Eventually, they reached the road and were soon parking in the Pex Hill car park.

'Phew!' Lester said, settling back in his seat. 'I didn't want to argue w_th him. Remember what happened the last time?'

'Too right. On the way back we follow the road. No more short cuts, okay?'

'Okay. Let's get some climbing done. I need to get changed.'

Thankfully, Lester had left the pink tights and the T-shirt with the *Lets Fuck While the Bacon Fries* message at home and was wearing a blue track suit. He was still too big to be a climber.

'Haven't been here for what, twenty years?' he said as they walked up the path leading to the quarry. He gestured with his hand. 'All this land is still protected by the green belt, so we did something right. Only thing that's changed is that the trees have grown up, and the place is greener. It used to be pink rock. Remember?'

'Just about.'

'Is it still owned by the Water Authority? Do they still try and stop you belaying to the railings?'

'No one bothers about that now. The big problem is that kids throw the metal palings from the fence into the quarry. It used to be rocks. Now it's six foot long metal spears.'

'That sounds dangerous.'

'Look,' Lester said. 'We need to get this green belt issue sorted. The future of the company depends on it. How are you getting on with the strategy?'

'I'm working on some ideas, Lester. Give me a chance.'

'Well, I'm counting on you, Martin.'

They walked for a while in silence.

'Blimey!' Martin said, wrinkling his nose. 'What's that pong!' A strange smell wafted on the light breeze.

Lester sniffed loudly. 'It's like a mixture of sweaty socks and blocked drains,' he said. 'Must be a maggot farm or something.'

'That's disgusting,' Martin said.

They walked through a wooden gate and down into the quarry. The smell went away.

'Look,' Martin said, 'I'll go and set up a top rope. You carry the sacks to the bottom down there.'

'So we're not soloing today,' Lester said with a grin. 'We used to do it all the time, didn't we? Wouldn't bother with ropes. Remember when John used to solo down into the quarry in his motorbike gear—leathers, boots and helmet?'

'Yes, I do. And with his rucksack on his back. The poser. Best to top rope until we get back into it.'

They top roped several routes, moving the belay along. Lester had to be hauled up in several places, and when he leaned back at the top to be lowered off, it took all Martin's strength to hold his weight.

At one point, as Martin moved the belay at the top, he met a young climber with long, shaggy, blonde hair and ripped jeans hanging around his arse.

'Hi, mate!' the lad said cheerily. 'Having a good time?'

'Yeah. Apart from the stink from over there.'

'Hah!' the climber said. 'That's where I work. You

wouldn't believe what goes on in there.'

'What are they doing, breeding maggots?'

'Might as well. I work in the pies.'

'That sounds a bit messy.'

'Not in them. I work where they make them. Everything goes into them: cows, horses, sheep. God knows where they come from. Makes you sick, it does. And the smell gets into your hair and your clothes. *Sizzling Sausages—locally produced quality* it says on the sign. What a load of crap. And it's minimum wage, zero hours, of course. Minimum conditions, minimum safety, minimum everything.'

'If it's that bad, why work there?'

'No choice. Hard up. Got a master's degree, but I can't get a normal job. Anyhow, have a nice day and enjoy your climbing.'

Martin looked over the edge. Lester sat on a large log, pouring tea into a cup from a flask. Something whirred through the air and crashed into the rock face nearby. Loud laughter on the other side of the quarry.

'Oh no, they're back,' the climber said.

'Oi!' came Lester's voice from below. 'Who's throwing stones?'

'Yeah?' came a kid's voice. 'And what are you going to do about it?'

'I'll tell you what I'm going to do about it!' Martin yelled. 'I'm going to throw you off there!'

He ran along the path at the top of the rock face, but brambles that snagged his legs soon stopped him. The stone-throwers had too much of a start, and he lost them.

He trudged back down to Lester.

'Heard anything more about Hardin?' Lester asked as they sat on the log drinking tea.

'He's been cremated and—'

'Cremated? That was quick. Sounds a bit dodgy to me.'

'Apparently he was involved with gangsters. His ex-wife wanted nothing to do with him.'

'I'm not surprised she feels that way. After what she went through. Why are gangsters involved?'

Martin sighed. 'Seems like he was involved in drugs. He owed them money.'

'Shit. We don't want to get mixed up in that, do we?'

'You're damn right we don't.'

'Good. You're supposed to be cutting down on stress. Hey, you know when we were driving in and you could see the back end of the Freeway Centre over by the motorway?'

'Yeah. It's pretty close.'

'Only a mile or so.'

'What happened to kilometres?' Martin asked.

'Same thing as happened to kilogrammes and metres.' Lester laughed and drained his tea. 'We're getting old, mate,' he sighed. 'I'm still stiff from that run and climbing at the wall. I had to rub Ibuprofen gel in everywhere just to be able to walk. It'd be easier to sit in a bath of it. Though it might get behind your foreskin like horse liniment. Remember that in the old days? The school changing rooms used to stink of it.'

Lester had been in the year above Martin, and he'd

looked up to him. Martin still remembered what the PE teacher had said when Martin won the mile: 'Good time, Bennett, but not a patch on Adams's record'. John had never tried hard at athletics or ball games; he'd been a true rebel. Then he'd realised that he was good at something—climbing. It must have given him a feeling of worth, being adopted and all.

Martin had looked up to John almost as much as he did to Lester—smoking dope, wearing the latest fashions, attractive to girls. He'd been a bit of a gangster, leading Martin on. Once they'd been caught shoplifting near the school. It'd been John's idea, but Martin was caught. He wouldn't implicate John, though. There'd been hell to pay. Martin would never discuss any of this with Lester.

'Remember that farmer?' Lester said. '"Put another leg over that fence and I'll give you both barrels!" Do you reckon it was the same one? Hey, did you see that item on the news a while back? Some hermit built a bungalow in the green belt, somewhere round here, and threatened a planner with a shotgun. Must be the same one.' He sipped tea and thought for a moment. 'Did you ever get anywhere with that funeral playlist?'

Martin looked at him. 'I did, actually.' He got out a folded sheet of paper from his wallet and handed it over. Lester scanned it.

'The Band? Love? They're a bit arcane. And why that Springsteen track? No one's ever heard of it. What you need is 'Born to Run', get their feet tapping. The Eagles, Captain Beefheart, that kind of thing.'

'It's what I like.'

'But you won't be there.'

'There won't be many there anyway.'

'Come on, I'll be there.'

They both contemplated this.

Martin looked up as a movement on the top of the quarry caught his attention. He dived onto Lester, pushing him off the seat. They sprawled in the grass as something thudded into the wood of the log. They sat in the grass, watching a fence paling still vibrating like an arrow shot from a longbow.

'Fucking hell!' Lester said. 'That could have killed me. Oi!' he shouted. 'You can stuff that up your arse for nothing and fuck off while you're doing it!'

The next paling hit Lester in the leg with a loud thunk and pinned him to the ground. There was a stunned silence for a moment, then the bleeding and screaming started.

CHAPTER THIRTY-ONE

The heat and the noise in the office were intolerable today, and Jane felt an attack coming on. Her heart raced, and her lower back was damp with sweat. She closed her eyes, leaned back in her chair and tried to breathe deeply and slowly.

After a few minutes she'd calmed down. She opened her eyes and went back to the file on her desk. It was a total mess. Sheets of paper, reports, folded plans, just shoved in any old way. A trained chimp could have done better.

She turned towards Ann Smith's desk. Ann was sorting through a pile of paper, head down, concentrating.

Jane slipped away from her desk, walked to the end of the corridor and into a room used as an archive—racks and racks of files and large cardboard boxes stacked up between the racks with hardly any room to move. She only just managed to squirm her way to the end of the room to a door with a sign reading *Mr S. Andrews Chief Environmental Health Officer*. The Environmental Health department had long ago moved to a different office down by the tunnel entrance. She opened the door—it was supposed to be locked. A large desk faced the door. A toaster sat on it, along with a plate with half of a Mothers Pride sliced, white loaf in its wrapper, a pack of Lurpak butter, a knife, a portable electric kettle, mug and tea bags.

She walked round the desk. A sleeping bag with a pillow on a roll-uppable foam mattress, the sort you took camping, lay on the floor. Another door led to a small toilet and bathroom. All chief officers had one. At the end, a shower. A damp towel was draped over a radiator, together with several pairs of drying knickers.

She looked in the desk drawers. Toiletries and underwear, female, filled one side. The other side held a fossilised bacon butty, rock hard and blue with mould. She moved it to one side with one finger. Beneath sat sheets of paper, yellow with age. She lifted one. On it was scrawled *Talks a good match but can she play?* Interview notes. A book: *Collected Contemporary Poems*. She flicked through, saw works by Seamus Heaney and Tony Harrison.

Jane returned the book and the papers to the drawer, taking care not to disturb the fossilised butty, and went back to the office.

'Ann, could you spare a moment?' she said as sweetly as she could.

'Is it important? I'm busy at the moment.'

Jane tried to control herself. She picked up a file. Ann also picked up a file. What was going on? 'Yes, it is important. Shall we go into the interview room?'

The room had once been the smoking room and, despite a coat of magnolia paint, the yellowness of the tobacco smoke had come back, giving the walls a seedy, unhealthy look. Jane opened her file and looked up.

Ann, pale and haughty, avoided eye contact. In her

mid-fifties with short grey hair, she dressed neatly but looked rather dusty. Jane had heard her co-workers calling her Eleanor Rigby behind her back. She was obviously an oddball who her previous manager had been happy to dump on the new mayoral team.

Still, you couldn't be a warm mother figure all the time. When the work demanded, you had to be firm. Like now.

'Ann, I asked you to have a go at this file and start to draw out the important documents. I gave you a copy of the quality toolkit. Have you read it?'

'Of course, I've read it.' When Ann spoke you saw glimpses of her missing front tooth. The kind of gap that most people would've had sorted with a bridge. Unless you were too poor. The council's policy was to pay minimum wage, but many were only just over the limit, making it difficult to make ends meet. 'It's just not the way we've done things up to now.'

'Well, I'm in charge, and we're going to do things properly. Look, when the system is up and running, it just makes everything easier. You know exactly where key documents are. And if members of staff leave, the new ones can easily pick it up. Don't you think that would be better?'

Silence.

Jane took a deep breath. 'Look, Ann,' she said. 'This is a direct instruction. I want this file organised according to the toolkit by the end of the week. If you don't obey this instruction, I will instigate disciplinary action. Is that clear?'

Ann looked away.

Jane resisted the urge to grab her face and turn it towards her.

'I'd prefer not to,' Ann said in a mild but firm voice.

Jane kept her gaze on her while Ann continued to look down. They sat like that for several long minutes. Ann pushed Jane's file to one side, then reached down, picked up her file and put it on the desk. She turned it so it faced Jane, then leafed through the pages until she reached the back cover.

'This is the MRA file for the Freeway centre project,' she said. 'They used a floor of this building at one time, and their archive files must've got mixed in with the council's. Someone made some notes here. See the initials. It was the mayor. Probably to jog his memory. There're notes in his handwriting all the way through. There were all sorts of rumours at the time that someone made a lot of money out of it, that the whole thing was corrupt. This file is dynamite.'

Jane reached over, but Ann held onto the file. She looked up and stared Jane straight in the eyes. 'Could we do a deal, Mrs T?'

'What sort of a deal?'

'Well, my job was done away with, and I understand that the council has a pot of money for people whose jobs have become not needed because of technological change.'Ann was remarkably alert and on the ball now. 'I'd like redundancy,' she continued, 'early retirement and five years enhancement. That should do it. In return, you can have this file.'

Jane laughed. 'Oh yeah,' she said, 'and you walk away pushing a wheelbarrow full of cash?'

'It's only what other people have got.'

Jane's mobile vibrated on the table.

'Jane?' Whitaker sounded irritated. 'My office. Now.'

*

'We need a result with the housing strategy.'

Whitaker wore a light grey suit with a white shirt and a light green tie. The suit fitted perfectly and the overall effect would normally be 'smooth political operator', but he was obviously worried about something. His face was a little too red and the lines in his forehead more pronounced than usual. Over his shoulder, Jane could see the Wirral on the other side of the Mersey: blocks of flats, low factories, warehouses; river green and slightly choppy.

'We can make a good case,' she said. 'There's a lot of pent-up demand for new housing. We can show that. The problem is finding the sites. The best ones are in the green belt.'

'There's been loads of discussion in the media recently about easing the controls, hasn't there?'

'Yes, but it's still this government's policy to protect it. You've got to have a good case.'

Whitaker leaned back in his chair. She held his stare for a little too long before she looked away. She'd skimmed through Ann's file, but there didn't seem to be anything obvious or concrete to implicate Whitaker in any wrongdoing. It would need another, more careful, reading.

'Look, Jane. Let's clear the decks and talk openly. I know we haven't exactly seen eye to eye. I know I'm an impatient kind of fellow, wanting everything done yesterday. But this is important to me.' He turned to look out over the river. 'Your assessment is due shortly, and to be honest up to now it's been difficult to be totally positive.' He turned back and stared her in the eye. 'So I'm giving you one last chance.' He pulled over his diary and made some notes. 'I want a robust strategy for taking fifty hectares of land out of the green belt and reallocating it for a mix of housing and commercial uses.' He put down his pen and smiled. 'This is your chance. If you're the kind of person I think you are, then you'll take it with open arms. I want the report on my desk within forty-eight hours.'

*

Jimmy Hughes completed the section on threats in the SWOT analysis in his business plan and put the pen down next to the set of handcuffs—standard police issue. He'd had to go to a sex shop in Manchester. He'd also bought some pills and a rubber truncheon and picked up a copy of the tide tables for the Mersey from a bookshop. The time was perfect. High tides in the late afternoon.

He texted Malone—*Mick Crosby beach 4pm Jimmy*—then put the phone down and gazed into the garden. He'd made a big thing under the threats heading of the need for IT support and staff training to keep ahead of the competition. The real threat couldn't be identified, of course.

The mobile's screen flashed a text from Malone: *Jimmy: Sorry can't make this afternoon. Bigger fish to fry, will be in touch Mick.*

Jimmy put down the phone and sat thinking for a moment. The gun. He'd lost the gun. It wasn't with the handcuffs. He'd checked the chairs, under the chairs, the sides of the chairs' cushions, the backs of the chairs' cushions. Not there. He'd have made a bit of a comical figure trying to subdue Mick Malone with a rubber truncheon.

'What're you going to do with that?' Malone would've said. 'Try and roger me with it? Come on, Jimmy, you're not a hard man. Put it away.'

Ah well. A huge wave of relief washed over him. It was true. He wasn't a hard man. Without a gun it would be impossible. Not worth the risk. And, in any case, a drowned man handcuffed to a statue would hardly look like an accident, would it? Most likely Malone would get bumped off by some rival or arrested and put away, anyway. So long as there were no links back to himself.

He picked up the file and leafed through to the spreadsheets. Do what he was good at. A bit of fine tuning would make things all right.

CHAPTER THIRTY-TWO

Totally shattered, Martin eased his tired frame back into bed, propped himself up on two pillows and sipped the mug of hot coffee. He'd carried a corner of the stretcher all the way down to the road and Lester was not a lightweight. The cops had turned up with the ambulance, but the kids who'd presumably thrown the fence paling were long gone. He'd not even got a good look at them. Then hours waiting in the Whiston Hospital waiting room only to be sent home with a 'Mr Adams is out of danger, but he is still unconscious. All we can do is wait.'

He drifted off and was woken by the phone ringing.

'Martin, it's Amy Hopkins. Lester's been moved to the Royal. There's complications with the injury. He's not going to walk or work again.' A pause. 'Look, someone's going to have to take over the urgent work. There's no one else; there's a meeting today at the mayor's office with Jane Trevelyan to discuss progress with the strategy. You'll have to go.'

'Hang on, Amy, you know Lester handled all the sensitive stuff himself. I—'

'There's no alternative, Martin. We'll go under if you don't do it. We'll all be out of a job. We're short-handed, and it gets worse. I've checked the books and the firm's on the brink of going pop.'

'But Lester kept all the files locked away or password-protected on his computer.'

'I've got the password.'

*

Martin put in the password: *fatbastard1*—applicable and self-deprecating. He scanned the computer files, cross-checking the most recent and appropriate documents. Not much to add to what Lester had already given him. He checked the e-mails. They only went back about eighteen months. Lester must have erased the older ones. A wave of despondency flooded through his body. Now why would he do that? E-mails counted as legal documents nowadays. What Lester needed was someone to rationalise his computer and paper filing systems, introduce a system of quality checks. That would do the trick. Martin leaned back in his chair. His head sank onto his chest.

Talking of tricks: a temporary technical assistant, a lad who only lasted a couple of months before he was sent back to the agency, had shown him how to retrieve deleted files from a computer's hard drive. After fifteen minutes of to'ing and fro'ing Martin managed to get up the e-mail record for the time when the problems that'd got Martin sacked were going on. He scanned through until he found what he wanted, then went into the financial records and scanned back to the same time. An interim audit report had been deleted but was recoverable.

Development Solutions had lost some key contracts and was in a cash flow crisis—about to fold. He skipped through and found the final annual audit report. No mention of any problems. He checked the Income and Expenditure sheets attached to the report. An item under income—*Feasibility work for strategic sites £200,000.* Two hundred thousand? For a bit of work by a tame consultancy? Twenty thousand would have been more appropriate. No invoice. Who had made the payment?

*

'Right, down to business,' Jane said. 'Coffee? Sandwich?'

It was the first time they'd met apart from the embarrassing do in the woods, and Martin wasn't sure if Jane Trevelyan recognised him. He wore his best suit, freshly polished shoes and had combed his hair, doing his best to appear as professional as possible. They met, just the two of them, in a small meeting room in the town hall annexe: grey carpet, one table, two chairs, magnolia-painted walls; maybe eight feet square, no window and not too different to the police interview room, the only difference being that the furniture in the cop shop had been a bit more battered and scruffy.

He accepted the cup of coffee and chose two sandwiches from the platter.

'By the way,' Jane said as she shuffled her papers, 'keep an eye on that Amy Hopkins. She's going to go far, that one. Bright as a new pin.'

'Yes,' he said. 'She's very helpful.'

'More than helpful. When we had that meeting to discuss the Irish Streets, she was masterful. Summed up the issues so well.'

'She was there with Lester, wasn't she?

'Yes,' Jane said. 'Lester played on his iPad the whole time. It was incredibly rude and embarrassing. I had to ask him to stop.'

'And neither of them left the room during the meeting?'

'No. Why do you ask?'

He didn't reply.

'Well,' she said, 'down to business. As far as I understand it, the brief was simple: to sketch out how housing can contribute to a long-term, economic strategy for Liverpool. Think off the wall and outside the box.'

'Sounds easy when you put it like that. I need to emphasise that whatever I say has not been agreed with Lester and is in outline only.'

'And everything I agree to here has to be confirmed by the mayor. How is Lester?' Her tone made it plain that she didn't think much of Lester.

'He's stable. It'll be several days before we know for sure.'

'Well, we've got to press on. The mayor wants action on this. Fire away.'

'Right. First, the obvious. Liverpool's early growth was based on the port and trade, then you had the decline of the empire, the rise of Europe, containerisation, post war light industry and especially cars. But we have the problems of lack of land for development, too many unemployed people and no money coming into the local economy. Ideally we'd be considering the Merseyside City Region rather than just Liverpool. There's more scope for development in the wider area.'

'Agreed. But that's political. We've got to work with what we've got.'

'Right. So we need to make the most of the city-centre retail offer, tourism, the port, financial services etcetera, etcetera. And we need more housing for owner occupiers with skills and education who pay their way. But where? Should we build on the green belt or on brownfield sites?'

'Have we not got enough housing land now that the moratorium is over?' Jane said.

'Nowhere near. Certainly not enough brownfield sites. Not the right ones, anyway.'

'Personally,' Jane said. 'I want to keep the green belt and the green wedges, but the mayor is under pressure on this.'

'The answer is not to do it piecemeal but to find the right big site, preferably a brownfield one.'

'We've looked everywhere with a fine tooth comb. There isn't anything. The Freeway development was the last big opportunity for that kind of thing. You were involved in that controversy, weren't you?' she said.

He took in his breath. Might as well lay it on the line. 'There was a leak,' he said. 'The developers were given vital inside information and made a lot of money. I was blamed.' He swallowed. 'I mean framed.'

'That doesn't surprise me,' she said. 'There's some funny business going on here. The mayor's under pressure from somewhere to release a lot of land in the green belt. He wants me to find a single site of fifty hectares.'

'About a hundred and twenty acres in old money?'

'Yep. At that rate, if we're not careful it'll end up as a free-for-all to concrete over the countryside and hollow out the city.' She paused, obviously still a little unsure how far to go.

'I couldn't agree more,' he said. 'But I'm not sure that it's straightforward graft and corruption. The politicians want to build houses and win votes. Whitaker's ambitious.'

'Well, he's given me an ultimatum on this to get it sorted or I'm out of a job. In fact, I've got a funny feeling that I'll be looking for a job whatever happens.'

'Funny,' he said. 'You could say that I'm in the same boat.'

Jane smiled. 'I've got something that might help you.' She lifted a worn, buff manila file from under her papers and handed it over. 'It's the MRA project file for the Freeway Centre project. It should've been destroyed, but someone put it in the archive for some reason. There should be stuff to implicate Whitaker in naughty goings-on, but I can't find it.'

He flicked through the file. 'You're supposed to hold onto project files for a certain amount of time, aren't you?' he said. 'For audit purposes? Can I hang on to this? I've got an idea. Give me a couple of hours.'

'A miracle worker, are you? Okay, ring me as soon as you have anything.'

He gathered his papers together and drained his

coffee cup.

'Do you often go running in the park?' she asked, smiling.

He felt his cheeks redden. 'Just started. Fighting a losing battle against the flab.'

'Well, when Lester wakes up could you inform him that wearing a T-shirt with a sexist and misogynist message emblazoned across it is not funny.'

He blinked.

'It's deeply sad.' She burst out laughing. 'Maybe we could go for a walk? Take the dog?'

Martin nodded. 'That would be nice,' he said. 'Yes, I'd like to do that.'

CHAPTER THIRTY-THREE

Steven Lightfoot was pissed off. Fucking pissed off. He'd had to start all over again on a job that was boxed off, in the bag, signed, sealed and delivered. He'd been sitting watching the lady's house now for at least an hour. He was not happy. In fact, he had the hump, the raving hump.

He ran through some paperwork, then noticed something out of the corner of his eye and looked up. She was outside, putting something in the back of the white four-by-four—a bag of golf clubs. She got in, drove quickly up to the junction and turned onto the main road with a squeal of brakes. Caught cold, he switched the engine on, but as he pulled out, a loud blast on a horn sounded, and a big wagon whizzed past, the driver gesticulating at Steven. He gave the driver the old one finger, but a long line of cars sat behind the wagon, and by the time he pulled out, Sheila was gone. He eased back into the parking space and thumped the steering wheel in frustration. It wasn't like the movies where Steve McQueen always managed to keep on the suspect's tail.

Then he remembered something. He checked his Smartphone and found a large golf course nearby.

Jane had got into the habit of standing in the small bedroom and checking the cars in the close and parked on the main road. Today she noticed the off-white van with SLL surveys written on the side. Ladders sat on the roof rack. It could be a plumber doing a job. Then she noticed someone in the driver's seat. The figure moved and the car started to pull out. A big lorry blared its horn and the van stopped. The driver made a gesture to the lorry driver, and she caught a glimpse of the van driver's face. It was him. She grabbed her car keys.

Sheila's car sat in the car park under a mature beech tree. Steven pulled into a vacant bay well down the line of cars. The golf course must have once been the grounds of a big house or something, with its mature trees and sandstone buildings—stables and the like. No sign of a house. Probably demolished.

He took a small rucksack with the gear and followed a path through woods. At the edge of the trees he stopped and scanned the course with his binoculars. He spotted a group in the near distance and heard a shout followed by cheers. Could be them. He took a circuitous route through the trees until he could see them. Sheila was teeing off. He quickly got the video camera from the rucksack.

Sheila gave the ball some wellie, the muscular power

obvious even from a distance. Like many big women, she was more powerful than she made out. He followed the group's progress, getting it all on tape. Oh, this was so perfect.

Walking back, he hummed a pop tune he'd heard on the radio that morning. Life was sweet. He noticed someone walking across the course and scoped the figure with his binoculars. Serendipity-do-dah! Two birds with one stone.

*

Something whizzed past Jane's head and crashed into the trees. Startled, she looked round. Nothing. Something whooshed past her head and splatted into the mud of the track. A large stone. She set off back the way she'd come as quickly as she could walk. Her breathing quickened. Her pulse raced. Sweat gushed from every pore in her body. Shit, the worst possible time for a panic attack.

Calm, now; calm. All you've got to do is tempt him into the trap.

'Go on, run for it!' someone shouted, hidden in the trees. 'Get rid of some of those pounds, fat arse!'

She recognised the voice and set off along the path that led to the top of the quarry.

CHAPTER THIRTY-FOUR

Martin took a mug of tea, the day's post and the copy of *The Guardian* up to the back bedroom, sat at the table and read the obituary again. He switched on his laptop and logged onto *UK Climbing*. Several posts had already appeared under *John Hardin RIP* from people who'd read the obituary. Two were from youngsters who'd heard his name but didn't know much about him. The You Tube video was mentioned. Martin walked to the wall and lifted the flap of wallpaper.

The investigation had hit another dead end. Originally, he'd had four suspects: Amy Hopkins, Lester Adams, Liverpool gangsters and the Irish variety. Amy and Lester had strong motives—Amy's father had been left to die by John, and he'd publicly called Lester a cheat. But they were the wrong size compared to the suspect on the escalator, and they both had alibis—they'd been in a meeting together at the time of his death and Jane had confirmed it. The trouble was that just about anyone who'd known John Hardin for any length of time—time enough to become a victim of his selfishness—would be a suspect. Neither the Liverpool gangsters led by Mick Malone nor the Irish lot would have murdered John without torturing the whereabouts of the money and the drugs out of him.

So who was the murderer? It was important to find out, for if he wasn't careful, Malone would torture him for the information. His daughter was under threat, and he couldn't go to the police. What a mess.

He checked the post: bills, flyers, bills, one official-looking letter. He opened it. The council's Environmental Health Officer had written with reference to a complaint from Mr Alan White and Sharon Mason—must be his neighbours—about playing loud music at unreasonable hours.

He stared at the letter for a few moments, then laid it down and walked to the window. A bin bag lay next to an empty whisky bottle in his yard. The bag had split, revealing an empty milk carton. He sat and took deep breaths until he'd calmed down.

A loud splashing noise, like a hosepipe filling a swimming pool, sounded clear and loud on the other side of the wall, then a loud wailing sound started up behind the opposite wall.

'I-eee-I-ee I will always love you! Oo-oo-oo-who-hoo!'

It was as if the splashing and the shrieking had been choreographed for maximum effect.

He put on *Visions of Johanna*, turned the volume to maximum and, knowing the Dylan song by heart, sang along to it as he went back to the table and spread out the Ordnance Survey map of Merseyside. One for the playlist? Or too much like a dirge?

'Ain't it just like the night to play tricks when you're trying to be so quiet ...'

He'd spent long hours trying to figure out what the lyrics meant. The lead guitar kicked in, the sound reverberating from the walls, while he followed the motorways with a finger. The Freeway Centre stood at the junction of two motorways. Just along from the junction, he noticed a large disused quarry: Wheathill Quarry. He googled it: once used for extracting sand and gravel for brickmaking; ceased in the Eighties; about fifty hectares. He pulled up some images on the screen: a fairly shallow bowl, areas of standing water, short sandstone walls, part of the quarry was used for waste disposal, about to cease. Ownership: Mersey Estates.

He laid a printout of the Garden City site in Kent on the table and compared it to the quarry site on the OS map. Roughly the same size. He sat up, suddenly wide awake. Why had no one thought of this before? Probably because part of it was a rubbish dump. But with a bit of landfill, grading and landscaping, it would be an attractive site. You might even get the government to pay derelict land grant to reclaim it. And structural engineers could do wonders with raft foundations. The right, big, brownfield site. He sat looking at the maps for a long time.

The cacophony from the other side of the wall stopped, and he turned his own music down. Remembering the photos of Debbie in the picture album in the farmhouse, he pulled across a sheet of paper and wrote down Debbie's birth date. He worked back twenty-five years, back to the fight with John. Things were slotting into place.

He rang the office, hoping Amy was still there. She answered.

'Hi, Amy,' he said. 'Look, this Irish Streets job, how was the contractor chosen?'

'The council's QS did it. Six firms were invited to tender.'

'Who were they?'

She read out the list. It didn't include anyone connected to Mersey Estates.

'So it was all above board?' he said.

'Of course. Why wouldn't it be? What are you implying?'

'Nothing.'

A long pause. 'How did the meeting go?'

'Fine, we're working on some ideas. We'll have some firm proposals soon.'

He put the phone down and sat thinking for a few minutes. Gayle's charge of corruption in the Irish Streets job was a red herring.

He sat back in the chair, reached for the project file and skimmed through, making some notes as he went. He compared the dates and times of the key events in the Freeway Centre project, marking them with coloured stickers. There'd been a lot of to-ing and fro-ing at the time between Lester, Benny Carter and Whitaker. He found a file note in Whitaker's handwriting—no initials but dated: *Strategic Sites feasibility study good result.* Martin went over to the wall and wrote a heading in felt tip: *LESTER'S EMAILS AND FREEWAY CENTRE PROJECT FILE,* then:

Whitaker wanted the secret report on the Freeway Centre site. Difference between agricultural and retail development value = millions

Lester's firm cashflow problems—about to go under

Lester's firm suddenly gets disproportionate fee for feasibility work from Whitaker's firm

Someone had betrayed him, and he knew who it was.

*

'The food's terrible in here,' Lester said. He sat propped up on a pillow, his leg encased in a huge plaster cast. He looked pale and tired.

The Major Trauma ward was surprisingly quiet even though it was visitors' time. Out of six beds, four were occupied—hopefully the occupants of the two empty ones had been discharged or moved on and not snuffed it. Two of the occupants were asleep, another was reading a book and the fourth, on the other side of the ward, had two visitors sitting by the side of the bed, obviously bored out of their skulls. Lester was in a small room off the main ward. He'd shut the door so they could talk in peace but could watch for the nurse through the glass pane in the door.

'Next time you come, could you bring a few items?' Lester said. 'Don't let the nurses see. I'll give you the money. A bottle of single malt, I'm not bothered what brand, just so long as it's a single malt. And some crackers, wholemeal, and a nice slice of cheese. I like that Spanish Manchego stuff. Have you tried it? Made from ewe's milk. Very tangy.'

'I thought you were on the wagon?'

'A man needs a bit of a treat at times like this. Keeps the spirits up.'

'You like your whisky and cheese, don't you?'

'The good things in life? What's the point of life if you don't enjoy the good things in it?'

A long silence. Martin avoided meeting Lester's eyes. 'I see the new hozzy's about to start,' he said at last. He took a grape from the bag on the bed and waited for Lester to respond.

'We should've won the contract to manage that.' Lester shifted his leg, encased in the huge plaster cast, to a more comfortable position. 'The bidding process was fixed. Shady deals in smoke-filled rooms.'

'I'd have thought you'd be good at that kind of thing.'

Lester frowned. 'What do you mean by that?'

'I mean the Freeway Centre report.'

'What's that got to do with building a new hospital?'

'Not much. It's got a lot to do with destroying someone's life and reputation, though. I looked up to you, Lester. You were my best friend. Like an older brother. But you needed money to keep you in your single malt whisky and nice cheese, so you betrayed me.'

Lester gazed at the plaster cast for several minutes. Martin waited, calm and patient. He fingered the automatic in his pocket—so small you could easily hold it without taking it out.

'I was at my wit's end,' Lester said. 'Everything was going to pot, to hell in a handcart. I'm not proud of what

I did. I wish I could turn back the clock, I really do, but I looked after you, didn't I? I tried to make up for it. Martin! Wait!'

*

Martin sat for a while in his car on the third floor of the hospital multi-storey car park. The pistol snuggled unused in his pocket, so small as to be like a mobile phone. You could hardly notice it. He felt utterly deflated, no energy left. The investigation was at an end, and he might as well pack it all in. It was leading him into dangerous places. Best back off while he had the chance.

Just one thing nagged him. John Hardin had been murdered on an escalator in full view of a CCTV camera. Whoever had done it must've realised this. Gangsters would've taken him somewhere quiet, tortured the whereabouts of the stash and cash out of him, then killed him and dumped the body.

Gayle was the key. Was she the murderer? She professed to have hated John with a bitter intensity. Martin couldn't see her murdering him, but she must know more than she was making out.

He started up the engine and drove down and out onto the street at the tail end of the rush hour—busy but not too busy. It was getting dark, and he had to drive round to Edge Hill to avoid the new hospital construction site with its road closures and diversions. He parked by Princes Park and walked the short distance to Gayle's house.

The door was locked. He banged on it with his fist but got no response. He was sure he'd seen a light flick off upstairs and sensed she was in. Maybe she thought it was bad people trying to break in. He hammered on the door again and shouted through the letterbox: 'Gayle, it's me, Martin. Open up! It's safe!'

Maybe she was entertaining a client. Ah well. Back to the ranch. He was starving hungry and could slaughter a pint.

*

The pub was almost deserted. Midweek. No sign of Robinson for once. He sat by himself with a pint of Pedigree.

It was too late to make a meal—only just enough time for a couple of pints then the chip shop. At this rate he wouldn't be able to skit anyone about being fat, he'd be a lardarse himself.

'Stand by your beds!'

Martin jumped. He'd been deep in thought.

Robinson wore the same maroon clown suit from the Seventies: pink shirt, pink tie, pink hanky in the top pocket, polished brown leather brogues. Had the pop turned him doolally? Always wearing a strange outfit like that on his days off.

He sat down next to Martin. 'How's it going, matey?' Robinson said with an air of forced jollity. 'I hear you've been busy.'

The piped music was low but loud enough to drown out their conversation. A couple of young lads sat at the bar, and a youngish man read a paper on the other side of the room.

'I hear you've been upsetting people,' Robinson continued when Martin didn't reply. 'Found out anything?'

Martin shrugged. 'Nothing much. Red herrings, dead ends. Dead herrings. Red ends.'

'Red ends. I like that. Sounds a bit dirty. Hey …' He nudged Martin's arm. 'I bet that barmaid's a goer.'

The middle-aged barmaid, who'd come round the bar to collect a few empty glasses, was quite tidy but getting on a bit.

'Can I give you some advice, son,' Robinson said, suddenly serious. 'Be careful. You're stepping on some important toes. People who stand to lose a lot of money and a lot of face. Both outside and inside the force. Do you want to share anything with me? Now's your chance.'

Robinson waited for a couple of minutes. When Martin didn't reply or even look at him, he drained his pint, shrugged his shoulders and left.

*

Branches covered with a layer of grass cuttings filled the bottom of the quarry, and that had taken a lot of the force out of the fall, but Steven was in pain. Fucking agonising pain. It felt like he'd busted a rib. Every time he moved or even breathed it hurt like hell.

He remembered reading a story in one of *The Wizards* they kept on the table for kids to read in the barbers in which an airman in the war had fallen from a burning bomber from 8,000 feet up over Germany. He'd landed in a gully filled with broken branches and covered in snow and survived. What was the opposite of serendipity? Sod's Law? The bitch probably thought he was lying lifeless in the quarry, little suspecting he was about to deal out retribution.

Jane's car nosed out of the close. Steven had parked behind another van, and in the impending darkness she didn't notice him. The village was rather busy in the early evening, and there was a bit of a queue at the cash machine. Steven had to hang back and pretend to examine the menu on the door of a Chinese restaurant. He couldn't move quickly anyway. He must have twisted an ankle in the fall into the quarry—as well as damaging his ribs. He had to limp hunched over and with his hood up—fucking Quasimodo. At least he would look completely different to his normal strutting big man self.

After Jane had collected her money, he watched her reflection in the window as she walked by on the other side of the road. Despite the pain, he felt a surge of pleasure. Revenge would be worth the risk. He followed her. She crossed to go into Sainsburys, and he had to hang back again. She stopped to talk to a man who looked old enough to be her dad. Steven winced as he heard their loud voices, something about 'organising that walk'. Joking and friendly. A bit too friendly. Who was this idiot?

He made a snap decision and decided to follow the man instead of Jane. She could wait. Steven had to know who this romantic interest was. The man went into a chip shop. It was nearly empty and he was quickly served. He came out with a package, and Steven crossed the road to follow him. The man walked halfway along the village street, then turned into a road with terraced houses on either side. Steven had parked his van there. He kept the man in sight and walked along the other side to the van. The man stood almost opposite, fumbling in his pocket for something and at the same time shifting the package—obviously not—from hand to hand. He didn't notice Steven unlock the passenger door of the van and slip quietly into the driver's seat.

CHAPTER THIRTY-FIVE

A big van had parked right outside the house with two wheels on the pavement. *SSL Surveys* adorned the side and ladders sat on the roof rack—most likely a gang of workies gone for a piss-up after work. Martin couldn't find his keys and the package of fish and chips was hot in his hands. He'd given in to temptation, but he didn't care. Eventually he found the keys in his back pocket. He never put them in his back pocket—too easy to lose in the pub. Shaking his head at his stupidity, he put the key in the lock, but as he opened the door, it crashed open into his face. He stumbled back. The keys flew to the ground, and chips spilled all over the pavement.

'What the fuck!' he shouted. He crouched down and turned to defend himself from what must be a mugger. 'Not again,' he whispered to himself.

DI O'Connor thrust his head into Martin's face, his own face unnaturally large. Fury contorted his features. His eyes bulged. His hair looked, and smelled, like steel wool.

What was he on? Martin instinctively flinched and dropped his head. O'Connor was the sort of bully who'd get up close to deliver a head butt, aiming to crush the cartilage of his victim's nose with the bone of his forehead.

'Listen here, Bennett,' O'Connor said through clenched teeth. 'I'll only say it once. Stop sticking your nose into things that don't concern you. You've upset some big cheeses in this city. I told you that to keep on would not be without risk. This is your final warning.'

Martin tried to stand up and step back at the same time, but his foot squashed a chip and he almost fell over.

'Careful, there,' O'Connor said. 'Some people just couldn't care less, throwing papers and chips on the street. Litter louts.' He paused. 'Look,' he said, calming down a little. 'Come inside.' He took Martin by the arm and manoeuvred him through the door, pushing it shut behind him with his foot. He shoved Martin down until he sat with his back against the hallway wall, then sat down beside him, as if they were building workers taking a break on a job. Except that it was so dark they could hardly see each other. Both were breathing hard.

'I suppose you know I'm being investigated,' O'Connor said at last. 'There're lots of people in this city who want to bury the hatchet—in my back. You make enemies within and outside of the force. Villains you've put away. Colleagues whose wives you've shagged. Bitter people in the force, jealous of your success. They've spread rumours about me. Unfounded rumours. I'm fed up with the whole shebang. I just want to retire to somewhere nice and warm—you know, like in the cliché?'

Martin got up on one knee.

'Where are you going?' O'Connor laughed. 'I haven't finished with you yet.' He grabbed Martin by the arm and pushed him back to a sitting position. 'John Hardin was your mate,' he said after a while, his mouth so close to Martin's face that flecks of spit spattered him as O'Connor spoke. 'I understand that. But pull back. You're in deep shit, and if you don't watch out it'll be over your head.'

He paused.

'I want two things from you,' he continued. 'Your mate, John Hardin, was involved in the theft of some property from some friends of mine. Namely, a holdall containing a load of cash and another containing a stash of cocaine. Cash and stash. I need these items as soon as, preferably sooner. Oh, and here's another cliché. I know where your daughter lives and where she works. Pretty girl, isn't she?'

Martin bristled. This bully needed a good punch in the gob, but he held Martin in a strong grip.

O'Connor let Martin go and got to his feet. He reached into a pocket and handed Martin a business card. 'Take this,' he said, 'and ring me if you get any information whatsoever on what we've just talked about.' He played the professional copper now. 'Otherwise I'll get you put away for perverting the course of justice.'

'Hang on,' Martin said.

O'Connor stopped and half turned.

'What you want, the cash and the stash,' Martin said, calm now, 'is hidden in a porta cabin in a farm next to the Freeway Centre. It's got an abattoir attached. They slaughter rustled sheep there.' A wild goose chase with a paranoid farmer armed with a shotgun was just what this idiot needed.

'I know it. Not exactly legal, but we were keeping

from busting them, thought it might be a front for something more serious.' O'Connor opened the door, letting in the glare from the white streetlights. He reached down and carefully plucked a chip from where it'd been caught in the front of Martin's coat. He popped the chip in his mouth. 'Soggy!' He grinned. 'I like my chips crisp. Remember that next time!'

CHAPTER THIRTY-SIX

The going wasn't as easy as Steven had imagined it would be, especially as it was getting dark now, and every time he put his injured foot down it hurt like hell. Every time he turned his upper body his ribs hurt as well. The trees were mature but not big enough to keep the undergrowth down, and he found it hard to avoid the clumps of brambles that tore at his legs while keeping track of the man in front and, at the same time, not be seen. Luckily, the man's shiny, steel-grey hair shone like a beacon. Did he dye it to look that way? Grecian 2000 in reverse? Asshole. Once Steven had heard the magic words 'stash and cash', he had to find out more. This could be a once in a lifetime opportunity. Revenge could wait for now. The way now cut mainly through ferns rather than brambles, and the man soon turned onto an old cart track that, after a few hundred yards, led to a farm.

At first sight the farm looked abandoned. Beyond, the tops of the Freeway Centre buildings peeked over a line of conifers. The man in front stepped over a broken-down fence that enclosed the woodland, skirted the conifers and walked towards the farmhouse. Steven followed. He passed abandoned farm vehicles and cars rusting into the ground, heaps of rubbish, plastic bags, chunks of plastic and pieces of rotten wood in piles with weeds growing around and through them.

A strong light from a mast high overhead lit up the farmyard. The farmhouse itself had several slates missing. Any paint had long weathered off the windows and doors, leaving the wood grey and the grain emphasised. Grass and small trees grew in the gutters. Green and orange streaks showed where rainwater had leaked down the brick walls.

The farmyard was relatively clear, and recent tyre marks marked the soil at the edges. Several barns and sheds flanked the yard, a couple of which might've been large enough to hide a vehicle in. One barn, constructed with concrete blocks and metal sheeting and obviously built more recently, was much bigger than the rest.

The man squatted down at the entrance to the yard, watching. Steven gradually edged forward until he was as close as he dared. The man moved towards the large building, stepping with difficulty over and through the debris. The gate into the overgrown front garden wouldn't budge, so he started to climb over.

A man in ragged and filthy overalls stepped out from the main door of the farmhouse. He held a double-barrelled shotgun. 'Okay, Mr snooperman,' he snarled at the grey-haired man. 'Put another foot over that fence, and I'll give you both barrels!'

Steven jumped up and stood paralysed for a moment, then he turned to run, but his injured foot gave way and he had to stop. A loud crack rang out—must be one of the barrels going off—followed by a cry of pain. The second barrel went off, and Steven felt a series of sharp thumps in the backs of his thighs and his arse cheeks. The pain was unbearable, far worse than his ankle and ribs. He ran in a desperate, stumbling sprint. If he got out of this alive he was never coming back.

*

Determined to have his fish supper, Martin returned to the shop and ordered again. When he got back to the house with his second lot of the night, he noticed that the van had gone and a car had parked in the space. A window slid down.

'Oh no,' Martin moaned at the sight of Malone's face—an inquisitive hedgehog under the spiky hairstyle.

'Come on,' Malone said. 'You can eat them in the car on the way. Just don't get any grease on the upholstery.'

'Way to where?'

'Where the stash is, of course. That is, if you want to see your gorgeous daughter again. O'Connor can go off on his wild goose chases, but this time there'll be no mistakes. Cute little thing, isn't she? I might have a bit of fun with her before I do what has to be done.'

Martin only just managed to control his anger at this disgusting threat to Debbie. *The animal!* Best go along with it for now. Bide his time.

Malone stuck his head out of the car window, looked up and down the street, then reached under the seat and poked the barrel of a pistol out of the window. 'Big, isn't it? he said. 'Colt 45. Standard issue in gangster films. I mean real gangster films like they used to have. Humphrey Bogart, James Cagney.'

'I'll get the wellies and the torches.'

They drove down Smithdown Road with low music playing on the radio.

'Geeks like you should keep out of things that don't concern you,' Malone said with deep contempt in his voice.

Martin could feel his own gun in the back of his pants, a toy compared to Malone's, but effective enough at close quarters. Malone was so contemptuous of him that he hadn't searched him. Hadn't brought Gobby— probably didn't want to share the cash and the stash. Over-confident.

'It would have saved us all a lot of bother if you'd just told us where it was in the first place,' Malone said as he turned the car into Gambier Terrace. 'Is this close enough? Have you finished the chips?'

He used a jocular tone, but Martin knew that once Malone got his hands on the stash any witnesses would be surplus to requirements. He'd hardly touched the chips. He folded the wrapper around them and put them at his feet.

Radio City News started, and Malone turned up the sound up. 'A prominent local solicitor has been found dead at the bottom of Helsby crag in Cheshire. Benny Carter was being investigated by the Law Society regarding charges of being involved in bank investment fraud and money laundering. Mr Carter acted for local soccer star Tony Gazelle, who was recently given a red card in the local derby. Fans have inundated this radio station with complaints about the bright orange shade of his latest hairstyle. A police spokesman said that they do not consider Mr Carter's death to be suspicious.'

Malone whistled and turned off the radio.

Night had fallen by the time they reached the cathedral quarry, and they had to use the torches to climb into the cave. At the pool, Malone stopped and shone the beam of his torch on the surface of the water.

'It's all right,' Martin said. 'It's only about six inches deep.' He walked on, keeping close to the wall. At the other side he shone the light back for Malone.

'No tricks now!' Malone shouted, his high-pitched voice like the squeaking of a bat in a cave. He pointed the gun at Martin. 'You just stay where you are.'

Malone stepped forward. He shone his torch on the water and felt around with a welly-booted foot. Something banged and clattered nearby, the sound echoing off the walls and rippling the surface of the water. A train. Malone recoiled with shock and stumbled. His wellies slipped, and he fell in the water with hardly a splash, disappearing quickly from view. He surfaced a few seconds later, yelling and thrashing in the water; the sound echoed around the tunnel walls.

'Help me!' he yelled. His mouth filled with water, and he coughed and retched.

Martin stepped forward and shone the light on the struggling man. This thug had threatened his daughter. He deserved to die. It would remove the threat from Martin's life, but, fuck it, the man was drowning. Martin reached forward. Malone grabbed his hand and pulled hard. Martin only just stopped himself from going in. Malone's hand slipped from his grasp and he was gone.

Martin shone the light on the water. The stream of bubbles ceased, leaving only rings of ripples that lapped at the sides of the tunnel. After a while they faded, and all was calm and quiet.

CHAPTER THIRTY-SEVEN

The Liverpool Wheel stood on one side of the large square in front of the Echo Arena. Martin disliked the arena; to him it was like a warehouse on an industrial park. The wheel loomed overhead as he approached. Streetlights lit up the thick, white-painted metal pipes and converged on the hub like the supporting arms of Yuri Gagarin's rocket in the Soviet film from the early Sixties—the arms that dropped away just before blast-off. The wheel had stopped but began to slowly rotate again.

The text from John had read, *Be at The Wheel 5 o'clock today if you want the truth.* He wasn't sure what to do. Somehow, John Hardin was alive. Unless it was someone faking the text. He looked around. The square was deserted. The 'murder' must have been faked somehow. But why? John Hardin acting selfish again, most likely. He felt a surge of anger against the man who'd ruined his life, and he fingered the pistol in his pocket. Unused as yet. It was wrong to hate that much; Martin realised that. After all, it wasn't that rare for someone's wife to have an infatuation for another man. It just felt so fucking bad if you were the husband.

A loud whistle echoed across the square. John had

always been good at those—two fingers in his mouth. He'd often used it to hail taxis or communicate on the rock face. He appeared from behind a kiosk, a big grin on his face. He wore fleecy tracksuit trousers and trainers or runners as they called them in Liverpool—handy for the getaway after robbing a post office. With a bobble hat pulled low on his head, he looked like a standard scally scouser.

'Martin,' Hardin said, the gap in his front teeth startling in the bright light. 'It's good to see you.'

'I never expected to see you again,' Martin said, trying to keep his voice calm. 'I would've gone to your funeral, but it was arranged rather quickly.'

'Ah, sorry about all that, kid. I had to disappear for a while. Here'—he motioned with a hand—'I've hired the private gondola. Only the best. We can rap in peace in there without anyone listening in. It's awesome how many rude people there are in this city.'

They got in and sat opposite each other. The doors shut and they slowly moved upwards. To one side stood the massive red-brick buildings of the Albert Dock, the great pillars and arches more like something from Ancient Rome or Classical Greece than the nineteenth century. Beyond, he could see the overbearing black prows of the new museums and the lighter-coloured Liver buildings, and the Mersey sweeping out to the Irish Sea. On the other side: the Anglican Cathedral looming over its surroundings, the spotlights already on; the Post Office Tower; hotels; brutalist concrete multi-storey car parks, and, right underneath, a red brick structure, an air shaft.

So that was how Hardin moved around like a ghost in the night.

'Great view, isn't it?' Hardin said. 'Like being on a wall in the Dolomites. You turning up like that out of the blue nearly put the kybosh on the whole thing. I had to wing it and only just managed to carry it off.' Pause. 'You see, there were too many people after me.'

'Like the police? I know what you were up to. Dealing in tainted drugs. The addicts dying in pain. Bollocks swelling up. Bodies rotting away. Proud of yourself, are you?'

'Collateral damage, mate. I didn't cut the stuff myself, did I? It's just one of those things. And as for the swollen bollocks, there are adverts for dick extensions all over the internet.'

'That's not funny.'

Hardin shrugged. 'Look down there.' He pointed. Martin leaned over. The people below looked like flies. 'Would you really feel any pity if one of those dots down there stopped moving?' Hardin said. 'There's hundreds of them dying at this moment in Syria and Iraq. If I said you could have fifty thousand quid for every dot that stopped moving, would you really turn it down? Or would you start thinking six dots equals three hundred grand, twenty dots a million. And it's free of income tax. For that amount, if you declared it you'd be paying fifty per cent tax on nearly all of it. So the way I'm earning, it doubles in value. Like magic.'

He stared out of the window for a long time, obviously thinking. Martin felt a strong urge to punch his stupid face. Knock his teeth out. He squeezed his hands into fists to try and control himself.

John turned to Martin, his face serious. 'That's a load of bollocks, isn't it?' He nodded at the window. 'Each of those dots is a human being, deserving to live and breathe just like you and me. I wanted out. I'd had enough. I was sickened by it all, but they wouldn't have listened. I need that money to start a new life where they can't catch up with me. I haven't got long with a fucked-up liver anyway.'

He coughed, then pulled a small, black box from his pocket, shook a little black sweet into his hand and popped it into his mouth. 'Imp?' he asked.

'No thanks,' Martin said. 'It's dirty money, though, isn't it? Who's in with you on this? Benny Carter? Gayle?'

'Ah, she's a good girl is Gayle. Did the job on the elevator and, all in all, was a great help. The thing is, the money is dirty, but if I don't use it they'll kill me and her. They'll do it anyway if they catch us. And good old Bluto was a great help too. Benny was a trooper too. You can only carry off a caper like this if you've got a good team around you ...' He paused. 'Pity Benny won't be around to spend his share.'

'Why did it have to be on a hospital elevator?'

'Lots of witnesses and a friendly doctor close to hand, old chum. Turned out well in the end, don't you think?'

'What about the poor soul who was cremated in your place?'

'He was a vagrant who was dead anyway. He wasn't in a position to care, was he? No one was hurt in all of this.'

'Well, I don't take too kindly to you threatening my daughter.'

'Your daughter? That wasn't me. It was Malone and O'Connor.' He stuck out his chin and took a defensive stance as if expecting an attack. 'Why would I threaten my own? Someone I love and cherish?' He laughed, the sound reverberating around the gondola.

Martin glared at him, realising the truth. 'Why you …' He leapt forwards, trying to get his fingers into Hardin's mocking gap-toothed face with one hand while pulling out the automatic with the other.

Hardin dodged the clawing hand, gripped the hand holding the gun and, with a deft twist, had it in his own hand. He pointed it in Martin's face. Martin stopped, infuriated. 'Just take it easy there, feller,' Hardin said. 'Calm down. What did you do with the holdalls, Martin?'

Martin stepped back. The wheel had reached ground level. The door slid open. 'They're in the tomb,' he said.

'What?'

'The catacomb. You have to pull hard to get the lid to move.'

'Oh, the Dracula tomb,' John laughed. 'Obvious when you know.' He handed the gun to Martin. 'Now be a good boy and put this little popgun away.'

CHAPTER THIRTY-EIGHT

'Jane? It's Martin. Look, I've got a proposition for you. Lester will be out of things for a long time, maybe for ever. There's complications with the injury. He's not going to walk or work again. He'll be in a wheelchair for the rest of his life. I won't lie to you, the firm's in financial difficulties, but I've got an idea for a big project. How would you like to come in with me and Amy Hopkins? A three-way partnership.'

Jane thought about it for a moment. 'Do I have to decide now?' she said.

Silence.

'No, sleep on it,' Martin said. 'I've still got something to sort out at this end. I'll ring you tomorrow morning to discuss it.'

Jane closed the mobile and leaned back in her seat, then she sketched out a resignation letter on the desktop. She would enjoy delivering it to Cath Benson and watch the smug smile disappear from her prim little face. She'd have to make sure that the Freeway project file—with copies of the relevant emails—was in a safe place for future reference. She corrected a typo and printed off two copies of the letter.

*

The departure lounge of Liverpool Airport was quiet at that time of night, just a gang of lost-looking students with huge backpacks. Martin was used to it being packed out with holiday-makers: scalls in football shirts, gold jewellery and tattoos off to Tenerife; middle class punters in sensible hats, M&S leisure wear, grey socks and sandals, off for a bird-watching holiday.

He looked around to check that no one was watching and slipped John the passport.

John stared at it for a moment, then opened it. 'Thank you, mate ...' he stammered, giving Martin a view of the gap in his front teeth. 'I ...'

'Take it,' Martin said. 'You can pass for me. So long as you keep your mouth shut. We're as ugly as each other now ... with all that money you can get a bridge put in that gap.'

John went off to weigh in the suitcases, giving Martin time to think about things. John Hardin had ruined Martin's life and been involved in a disgusting drugs trade, but he'd been sickened by it. He might be faking the remorse and desire to change, but Martin didn't think so. In any case, he'd be out of Martin's life along with his lying moll.

Gayle walked over to where he stood. She wore a white dress that showed off her figure and golden blonde hair and skin to great effect. She must be spending time in a tanning salon. She slid a hand around his waist. He could feel her hips. She held his hand, pressing her thumb into the top of his index finger.

'Will you be okay?' Martin felt aroused by her, which made him angry with himself. She'd betrayed him and he'd most likely never see her again.

She turned, then laughed. 'Cheer up!

He grunted something and turned away.

John had almost finished weighing in. The invite to board the flight flashed on the screen overhead.

She put her mouth to Martin's ear. 'We'll always have Toxteth, darling.'

By the time Martin turned to tell her it wasn't funny, she'd gone.

*

'For fuck's sake,' Martin murmured under his breath. He still had the gun in his pocket. It hadn't been used, but he'd still get into trouble if the cops found it on him.

He heard a shout. Robinson sat in the dropping off area, leaning out the window of an unmarked grey Ford Focus. 'For a moment there, I thought you were going to do a runner on me!' Even from ten yards away Martin got a view of yellow-stained, blackened and gold teeth and remarkably pink gums.

He walked over, and they both turned to watch the Easyjet roaring overhead.

'Boy, have you been helpful,' Robinson said when the noise died down. 'Micky Malone found drowned in a tunnel next to a holdall with a stash of drugs. Chief Inspector O'Connor gunned down by a mad farmer. A search of the farm reveals a sheep rustling and fake food scam. That's three positives for me, Mr Bennett. I don't think we'll bother with your Mr Hardin. Little fish in a big sea. Hooking him would make me just that little bit too much of a success, even at my age. They might even keep me on, when I can go out now in a blaze of glory and enjoy spending my pension. I've had enough, mate.' He spat onto the pavement.

'In the movies, Martin, this would be the start of a beautiful professional friendship, but it isn't the movies, is it? So you can fuck off, and I don't ever want to see your mug again.' He grinned. 'Unless it's in the pub!' The car window shot up and the Focus roared off with a scream of tyres.

*

It was dusk and the lights were going on all over Liverpool. Jimmy Hughes contemplated the view. And what a view. The big wheel all lit up and revolving slowly. Liver buildings, Albert Dock, Pierhead. All virtually obscured by the brash new buildings. Should they go on the model? No, it was set in 1956 and anyway most of the new buildings were crap. World Heritage site? My arse.

He pressed the button on the remote and set the train going. He watched it glide along the elevated railway then down and into the tunnel. The news had been good. Mick Malone found drowned in a pool in one of the tunnels next to a holdall packed with drugs. No money but hey-ho, win some, lose some. A blood sacrifice for the people on the other side of the pond. Now he could go completely legit and build up Mersey Estates. Who knew where it might lead? Today Merseyside, tomorrow the world! He felt a surge of adrenaline, something he'd not felt since he was a dreamy kid.

He walked over to the desk and picked up the business plan, all tatty and dog-eared. He could complete it. The only threats he would face now, the only risks to take, would come not from dangerous psychos but from recessions, competition and exchange rates.

The train came out of the tunnel and he pressed the toot button.

CHAPTER THIRTY-NINE

A new banner had been stuck across the huge artist's impression on the hoarding outside the hospital.

Work on your new hospital starts soon!

Martin and Jane stopped to stare at the sign.

'Come on,' Martin said. 'We've got a busy day. We've got to meet Jimmy at the Wheathill site for twelve.'

They walked on. Another hoarding came into view, even bigger than the first one. James Whitaker's huge face, tanned and with a Hollywood smile, beamed down at them, like Big Brother but not obviously menacing. Below the face, it said in huge letters.

Vote Whitaker! Justice and Freedom Candidate!

'I hope you've got that project file well tucked away,' Martin said. 'That's our public liability insurance.'

'Oh yes. Safely stored where the sun don't shine. And public liability is for clients and members of the public. For us it's personal liability.'

He laughed. 'So long as it covers the risk. And it might provide an opportunity rather than a risk, who knows?'

She laughed and squeezed his hand, They walked on towards the entrance.

A group of smokers huddled together under a sign on the wall above them that read: *Let's not smoke outside the new hospital!* No doubt the architect's brief for the new building would've included the requirement to design out smoking. Restrict access to the outside without getting clearance first would be the best way—like in an open prison.

They followed the corridors under fluorescent lights. Martin noted the messages set into the blue lino on the floor: *Compassion, Commitment.*

At the clinic they had to wait five minutes, then he was ushered in to have his weight checked and his blood pressure taken. The young male doctor had grown a small goatee beard in the month since Martin's last visit. Iranian, maybe? Father escaped from the revolution? Family of doctors? He was certainly smartly dressed: grey suit trousers, crisp white shirt and red, ox-blood, pointy-toed shoes.

'Ah, Mr Bennett, how are you?' The doctor greeted him with a warm smile. 'Good. And is this your lady friend? Pleased to meet you. Mr Bennett, your blood pressure is right down into the normal range. Have you had a restful month? Chilling out? Gentle exercise? No stress?' He looked Martin up and down. 'You're certainly looking better. I think we can defer the operation indefinitely. Let the change in lifestyle and medication do their work. No need to take unnecessary risks, eh?'

'Exactly. So what happens next, doctor? What's the prognosis?'

'The prognosis is good. Keep taking the tablets. Eat healthy food. Get lots of exercise.'

'I've certainly brushed up on my gardening skills

recently. It's given me a whole new lease of life.' He didn't have a garden but what the heck.

'And the drinking? Moderate, I hope?'

'Tell the truth!' Jane said.

Martin turned at the painful dig in his ribs. Jane's expression held just a little bit too much self-righteousness.

ACKNOWLEDGEMENTS

Tahlia Newland for editing.
Kevin Berry for proof reading.
Catherine Wilson for formatting.
Ned Hoste of 2H Design for the cover design.
Paula Trewin for beta reading and support.
Ian Grady for beta reading and humour.

THANK YOU FOR READING

If you enjoyed reading this novel, please consider leaving a review on Amazon. It's also available as an e-book.

You can contact me direct to tell me what you thought of *Not Without Risk*:
Post on my Facebook page:
www.facebook.com/PeteTrewinAuthor
E-mail me via my website:http://www.petetrewin.com

My website has information on forthcoming novels and some background to the north of England settings in my books. There is also information on my interests which range from conservation of historic buildings to rock climbing.

Find more great books in the bookshop on the AIA Publishing website: http://www.aiapublishing.com

www.ingramcontent.com/pod-product-compliance
Lightning Source LLC
Chambersburg PA
CBHW030237030426
42336CB00009B/140